Toward a Resilient Metropolis
The Role of State and Land Grant Universities in the 21st Century

Arthur C. Nelson
Barbara L. Allen
David Trauger
Editors

metropolitan institute
at Virginia Tech

MI Press
Alexandria, VA

About the Metropolitan Institute at Virginia Tech

The Metropolitan Institute at Virginia Tech conducts basic and applied research on national and international development patterns, focusing on key forces shaping metropolitan growth such as demographics, environment, technology, design, transportation, and governance. It seeks to expand knowledge in urban and metropolitan affairs in order to improve policy and practice, and educate the general public on important issues facing communities. The Metropolitan Institute shares knowledge through events, presentations, publications, a website and media outreach.

The Metropolitan Institute's current research program includes five major initiative areas and objectives:
The New Metropolis - explore changing regional growth, demographics, land-use and transportation patterns
Fair Growth - examine regional equity issues such as fair share housing, environmental justice, and transportation accessibility and study their impact on metropolitan growth patterns and policies
Green Regions - investigate ways to create environmentally sustainable regions through better building and community design
Smart Governance - understand how technology can improve governance and enhance citizen participation in the planning process
World Cities - assess how major metropolitan areas fit into the world economy and the world system of cities

The Metropolitan Institute was founded in 2001 and is part of Virginia Tech's College of Architecture and Urban Studies.

Recommended bibliographic listing:
Nelson, Arthur C., Barbara L. Allen and David L. Trauger, eds. 2006. Toward a Resilient Metropolis: **The Role of State and Land Grant Universities in the 21st Century.** Alexandria, VA: Metropolitan Institute at Virginia Tech,

ISBN: 0-9778092-0-X

Cover photo by Arthur C. Nelson
Sculpture by Marcel Gagnon: "Le Grand Rassemblement," Sainte-Flavie, Quebec
Layout by Jessica Hanff, Washington D.C.
Printed by Sheridan Press, Hanover PA.

Contents

Foreword
The New Responsibility for State and Land Grant Universities

In May 2005, a unique national symposium, ***transForm: the River Farm Conversations for a Sustainable Metropolis***, was held at George Washington's farm along the Potomac River south of Alexandria, Virginia. The symposium, sponsored by Virginia Tech, was planned and organized by faculty from three academic units each in different colleges: Arthur C. Nelson (the Urban Affairs and Planning program in the College of Architecture and Urban Studies); Barbara Allen (Department of Science and Technology Studies in the College of Liberal Arts and Human Sciences); and David L. Trauger (the Natural Resource program in the College of Natural Resources). Thoughtful and intellectually provocative papers from six nationally recognized leaders and scholars framed the conversations: Frederick R. Steiner (University of Texas – Austin), David W. Orr (Oberlin College), David J. Hess (Rensselaer Polytechnic Institute), Janice Cervelli Schach (Clemson University), Ann Forsyth (University of Minnesota), and Frank Fischer (Rutgers University).

The charge of the symposium was to begin conversations on how to transform graduate education, research, and outreach to attain a sustainable metropolis over the next generation and beyond. Although initially organized for the benefit of academic programs in three colleges (Architecture and Urban Studies, Liberal Arts and Human Sciences, and Natural Resources), insights transcend all academic, research, and outreach units of Virginia Tech. And although the conversations were initiated with emphasis on Virginia Tech's presence in the northern Virginia/Washington, D.C. region, known as the National Capital Region, the view was broadened to provide for a global perspective.

For two-and-a-half intense days of presentations, dialogue, "cognac conversations", and reflective walks along the banks of the Potomac River, the issue of a sustainable metropolis was our focus. One theme that was repeated throughout was the challenge not only to transform current pedagogies, methodologies, theories, and even philosophies but to direct them to achieve a metropolis that is not only sustainable but resilient, able to learn and correct and renew in the face of change. The River Farm Conversations identified Virginia Tech's unique "power to convene," and issued a call for it to transform graduate education, research, and outreach to achieve a resilient metropolis. The power to convene and the call for transformation are integral aspects of both the historic purpose and the future role of state universities in general and land grant universities in particular.

The unique role of land grant universities was especially considered. Vermont Representative Justin Smith Morrill's land grant legislation was signed into law as the Morrill Act by President Abraham Lincoln on July 2, 1862. The Morrill Act was designed to donate federal land (30,000 acres total) to each state and territory as an endowment to establish at least one college in each state. Its stated purpose was to make higher education available to the citizens in every state in the nation, especially members of the working class, who would obtain a "liberal, practical education."

Throughout his service in Congress, Senator Morrill continued to advocate for land grant colleges and their role in serving state citizens. In 1890, the Second Morrill Act was passed and specified that states that maintained separate colleges for different races had to propose a just and equitable division of the funds to be received under the act. This act established 16 black land grant colleges throughout the South, known as the 1890 land grants. The act also provided for education in some of the arts and all of the sciences, thus allowing for the expansion of the higher education system. In 1994, 29 Tribal Colleges were added to the land grant system.

Since the 19th century, the land grant universities have expanded (1862, 1890, and 1994) but have maintained their mandate for openness, accessibility, and service to state citizens. They have shared the traditional tripartite mission of teaching, research, and service (extension) through the 20th century. Although many of the 105 land grant institutions are among the ranks of the most distinguished public research institutions and graduate 60 percent of the nation's doctoral degrees, the goal of meaningful, liberal, and practical education for citizens also is being realized through the land grant institutions.

The 21st century requires changes in higher education, and the land grant colleges and all other universities have a unique responsibility to respond. At Virginia Tech, this responsibility is addressed through the Graduate School's initiative called Transformative Graduate Education. It is framed by the four cornerstones of knowledge, leadership, scholarly inquiry, and social responsibility. The chapters in this book expand on these themes to include sustainability, resilience, restoration, healthy communities, regional perspective and local action, social movements, community design, environmental protection, and collaboration in the context of reshaping America's and the world's metropolitan regions.

Karen P. DePauw
Mark McNamee

Acknowledgements

This book is a product of a symposium convened May 4-6, 2005 called ***transForm: the River Farm Conversations for a Sustainable Metropolis***. Our first acknowledgement goes to Karen P. DePauw, Virginia Tech's Vice Provost for Graduate Studies and Dean of the Graduate School, initially for challenging the editors to rethink the nature of graduate education and research conducted by state and land grant universities in metropolitan areas and then for underwriting the event.

The River Farm Conversations were held at George Washington's River Farm on the Potomac River, now headquarters of the American Horticultural Society. Acknowledgment goes to the AHS for enabling use of its facilities and especially to Trish Gibson whose management of on-site logistics helped make the experience extraordinary.

Three colleges were involved in many ways to assure participation of key faculty members and lend logistical support. Acknowledgements are due to: Paul L. Knox, Dean of the College of Architecture and Urban Studies; Jerome A. Niles, Dean of the College of Liberal Arts and Human Sciences; and J. Michael Kelly, Dean of the College of Natural Resources. Three other administrators were key to making the event successful including: John Randolph, Director of the School of Public and International Affairs – who also assumed important leadership in synthesizing the conversations; Valerie Hardcastle, Director of the Graduate Program in Science and Technology Studies; and Robert Bush, Associate Dean of the College of Natural Resources. We also acknowledge Ronald M. Kagawa for initial leadership in planning the River Farm Conversations.

Events such as this are not successful without the help of staff. Sophie Cantell Lambert helped with numerous organization logistics including preparing the proceedings that ultimately led to this book, as well as for being the event's scribe. Jessica Hanff provided editing assistance and took charge of the book's layout. Carol Bell provided professional editing guidance. A special acknowledgement is due to Myriam Lechuga for coordinating the colleges, River Farm management, catering, travel logistics, accounting, and all the other behind-the-scenes things that assured success.

Arthur C. Nelson
Barbara L. Allen
David L. Trauger

Introduction: Toward Metropolitan Resilience

Arthur C. Nelson, Barbara L. Allen, John Randolph, and David L. Trauger

According to a special issue of *Scientific American* (2005), the first decade of the 21st century witnessed a tipping point: For the first time in history, more people live in metropolitan areas than outside them. The world's population, which doubled from 3 billion in 1960 to 6 billion in 2000, is projected to reach about 9 billion by 2040 before leveling off. Two-thirds of the world's population will live in metropolitan areas. This will put additional stress on the world's ecosystems, not to mention economic and political systems. Where one agricultural worker today feeds herself (women are the primary source of farming in the world) and one urban dweller, by 2040 she will need to feed two urban dwellers.

Scientific American's special issue goes on to note three other trends. First, the world's natural systems are already stressed. Since about 1960, global carbon dioxide emissions exceeded the capacity of the oceans and the land to absorb them and even the most optimistic projections do not show a tapering off of emissions until about 2040 – at more than six times the earth's capacity to digest it.

Second, Earth's plant and animal resources are becoming increasingly stressed. The rate of extinction of life is roughly 1,000 times greater than in the absence of human activity that drains wetlands, clears forests, and pollutes the atmosphere. Yet, one activity that is especially aggressive in facilitating extinction – clearing tropical forests for agriculture – is also enormously inefficient: Roughly half of the planet's tropical forest or seven million square kilometers have been cleared for agriculture but only two million square kilometers have become productive.

Third, economic systems are becoming increasingly stressed. The primary fuel for global economic development has been oil but beginning some time in this decade the global supply of oil will begin to fall because all major oil reserves have already been discovered. This is occurring just as China and India are achieving economic growth rates comparable to industrialized nations; per capita incomes are expected to rise to levels just short of western industrialized nations in a generation. Already, China's energy use is growing at 9% per year and it is out-bidding American buyers for such staples of economic development as steel and cement.

Development in the US between now and 2040 will further stress systems (Nelson 2006). Roughly 100 million new Americans are expected (more than a third from immigration) along with about 60 million new jobs. Two million homes will need to be constructed each year and non-residential construction may top two billion square feet annually. More than half of all non-residential space existing in 2000 will become obsolete and will need to be removed or rebuilt – lest it goes vacant. New development is projected to exceed in volume two-thirds of everything built today, at a cost of more than $50 trillion.

It is against this backdrop that *transform: The River Farm Conversations for a Sustainable Metropolis* was convened in May 2005. One purpose of the River Farm Conversations was to hear about emerging trends and prospects for transformative education, research and outreach under the umbrella initially called "**the sustainable metropolis.**" Another was to discuss the role of Virginia Tech's programs in the National Capital Region in advancing the transformation. The special focus was on how the three colleges sponsoring the symposium could reposition themselves for the 21st century. Those colleges included Architecture and Urban Studies, Liberal Arts and Human Sciences, and Natural Resources. Six invited scholars prepared papers and led conversations around various themes common to all colleges – and more broadly to the university itself. The conversations quickly expanded to include all disciplines engaged in shaping the built and natural environments even if indirectly, and all institutions of higher education.

Frederick R. Steiner posited the notion of "metropolitan resilience" where communities and regions learn how to prepare for, respond to, and embrace change, and in the process enhance social capital, create knowledge capital, and protect natural capital. He offered two examples of how universities have helped communities tackle these issues of growth and change on a regional scale: the involvement of Arizona State University in Greater Phoenix 2100 and the involvement of the University of Texas-Austin in Envision Central Texas. Scenario formulation became an important element of these processes especially the latter.

David W. Orr offered an impassioned view of the forces and drivers of future metropolitan change, especially energy and climate, and our technical and analytical capabilities, including green buildings, biomimicry, energy accounting, and GIS. Orr stressed that universities and foundations must position themselves in the global economic and information change that is remaking higher education using the power to convene to initiate a larger discussion about the future of governance relative to the challenges of transformation. Transformation must be the product of rethinking the conventional wisdom of higher education in terms of disciplinarity, audience, modes of delivery, and governance.

David J. Hess first stressed the synergistic development of state, university, and industrial clusters, often referred to as the "technopole" or "triple helix," related to science policy and economic development. Second, while such clusters now focus on IT (information technology), BT (biotechnology) and more recently NT (nanotechnology), there is considerable potential for developing ET (environmental technology) as a stimulus for economic development and environmental improvement. Third, justice and equity are critical elements of sustainability and the process of globalization is a critical force in determining our future industry, economy, environment, and governance. Fourth, social movements are critical mechanisms toward transformation of manufacturing, energy, agriculture, workplace, health, and home. Finally, these processes have a global dimension, but it is their local manifestation at the neighborhood, community, and metropolitan scale that will lead to transformation and the university is strategically positioned to facilitate change through education, research, and outreach.

Janice Cervelli Schach discussed the development of the Restoration Institute at Clemson University, including the thematic concept of restoration and its diverse applications: restoring resources (natural, historic, cultural), restoring minds and bodies (health, housing, recreation), and restoring economies (tourism, industrial clusters). She went on to describe restoration clusters in South Carolina and the response of the new Institute in developing faculty teams in Preservation and Conservation, Advanced Materials and Methods, Urban Ecology, and Healthy Communities and Buildings. The teams have developed degree concentrations, outreach programs, and partnerships. The Restoration Laboratory with two locations near Charleston, provides an off-campus focus for the Institute's activities.

Ann Forsyth (presenter) and Gretchen Nicholls (co-author) addressed the issue of affordable housing as an important component of the sustainable metropolis. She described the development of the University of Minnesota's Metropolitan Design Center which she directs. She then used the experience in Minneapolis in converting "left-over" places to affordable housing (the Corridor Housing Initiative) to illustrate how the university can assist the process through visualization and facilitation. She observed that the conventional approach for big and bold responses to the development challenge of the next three decades is large-scale development emphasizing big land areas. But "is there an alternative path that can rebuild the city in a comprehensive way but in small places?" She answers by noting that "left-over" places are inherently small and dispersed but in aggregate may offer the best opportunity to rebuild cities one neighborhood at a time.

Frank Fischer brought a strong social, participatory, and normative approach to the discussion, critiquing the fact-based, positivist dimensions of conventional planning and professional programs. His alternative approach he calls "civic ecology," which encourages citizen participation and deliberative decision making by civic stakeholders to create a common ground for envisioning desired future conditions for sustainable communities and ecosystems. Such an approach can produce collaborative dialogue to help close differences among stakeholders, tap local knowledge, and build common understanding. The university can foster civic ecology through public environmental education, community-based environmental research, establishment of citizen juries, and other means that could be facilitated by Cooperative Extension at land grant universities.

On reflection, the River Farm Conversations were filled with bold ideas on how our world may be transformed into a more just and sustainable place. They ranged from alternative practice ideas, such Forsyth's infill housing ideas, to large scale regional planning initiatives such as those proposed by Steiner. There were also synergies suggested, such as Hess' idea of university/industry/government partnerships around manufacturing, energy, health care, agriculture and banking. Clearly, grand ideas by major scholars were put forth on how a region can become sustainable in a number of sectors, using the term "sustainability" broadly. But after viewing such large scale planning proposals as Steiner's for the Austin area, the questions remains: How can these proposals become reality? To start with, as Fischer observed, we need to engage in dialogue with all the interests. Without informed and constructive dialogue making metropolitan areas resilient may not be possible. One wonders, for example, the extent to which the lack of "civic ecology" contributed to losses associated with Hurricane Katrina in late 2005 – which occurred just months after the symposium.

Metropolitan areas must not only become regions of sustainability but ones of resilience – and perhaps they must first learn to be resilient (see Vale and Campanella 2005). What is the role of universities in facilitating this? As DePauw and McNamee note in their foreword and later in their afterward (with Randolph), the central role of state and land grant universities must not be understated. State and land grant universities have the special charge not only to educate and conduct research but to engage civil society. The days of agricultural extension offices located throughout every state may be history but the model of the university extending itself into the fabric of everyday life across regions is as important now as it ever was. Federal land grant universities are charged especially with engaging communities but this charge is becoming accepted broadly by all state institutions of higher education. This can be accomplished through their collective *power to convene*. This power can be expansive. State and land grant universities may convene scholars and students in traditional, professional, or executive education modes leading to degrees, certifications, or simply expanded awareness. They may convene researchers directly and through networks to address issues of concern by federal agencies and national research sponsors. And they may convene scholars, professionals, public officials, and leaders in government, business, and interest groups as part of its outreach function. No other institution enjoys this collective power. With this power to convene state and land grant universities have the responsibility to forge the resilient metropolis.

References

Nelson, Arthur C. 2006. *ReShaping America*. Chicago: American Planning Association.

Scientific American. 2005. Special Issue: Crossroads for Planet Earth. *Scientific American* 293(3): 44-115.

Vale, Lawrence J. and Thomas J. Campanella. 2005. *The Resilient City: How Modern Cities Recover from Disaster*. New York: Oxford University Press.

Toward a Resilient Metropolis
The Emerging Role for Universities

Chapter 1
Metropolitan Resilience:
The Role of Universities in Facilitating a
Sustainable Metropolitan Future

Frederick Steiner

For the first time in human history, more than half of us live in cities. We live in what several commentators dub the "first urban century." But the urban form of this century is unlike cities of the past. In much of the developing world, informal settlements occupy vast tracts of land on the periphery of cities. In the developed world, suburban sprawl dominates. That sprawl tends to be horizontal across the landscape with single-family houses and lower-rise commercial and retail developments in North America. In Europe and Asia, suburban sprawl is more vertical and high-rise in form.

The spatial extent of this sprawling suggests that we actually live in the "first metropolitan century." Contemporary urban settlements are a combination of traditional cities with agglomerations of suburban sprawl and/or informal settlements. Traditional cities depended on their rural surroundings for food and water. Small towns and farms forged economic and social connections with cities.

In this new metropolitan century, this symbiosis continues, with increased pressure on the use of prime farmlands, the quality and quantity of water sources, and the character of small towns. In addition, growing metropolises require open space areas for recreation as well as places to dispose waste. In many ways, the character of a metropolitan region is forged by the combined qualities of its built environment and its natural environment.

The challenge especially for large metropolitan areas is to prepare themselves to be resilient to change and to repair themselves when damage occurs – especially to the environment or their local ecosystems – and to define universities' role in facilitating a sustainable metropolitan future. The assumption is that metropolitan areas that are knowledge creators will be more resilient to change than those that are knowledge importers, and metropolitan-based universities have a central role in creating the knowledge to make their regions resilient.

To explore this topic, I first explore the drivers of global change that are likely to affect metropolitan regions in the 21st century. Second, I discuss the concept of resilience as a means for coping with these changes. I argue that resilience is related to enhancing social capital, expanding knowledge capital, and protecting the natural capital of a place. Third, I offer examples from Phoenix and Austin that suggest roles for metropolitan-based universities in resilience scholarship and practice.

Drivers of Landscape Change

Change does not just happen. A variety of economic, social, and technological forces *drive* change. What drivers of change will influence landscapes around the world in the 21st century? Some possibilities include:

- Population dynamics and consumption
- Urbanization
- Connectivity and networks
- Technology, economics, and politics
- Culture and the arts
- Education and human services
- Global and regional environmental processes

Population growth and migration will change the planet's demographic structure. At the beginning of the 20th century, Earth was home to some two billion inhabitants; now it has 6.3 billion. The United Nations projects that the world's population will plateau at 9.4 billion by 2050, then creep up to 10.4 billion by 2100 (Barrett and Odum 2000; United Nations 1998). Considering potential death rates, the prediction translates into some 12.6 billion more people joining us over the next century (Brand 1999).

Population growth drives change because everyone requires water, food, shelter, clothing, and energy. However, levels of consumption vary. The ecological footprints of some communities are larger than others. The United Nations notes that globalization tends to separate the costs from the benefits because "consumers derive goods and services from ecosystems around the world. . . . This tends to hide the environmental costs of increased consumption from those doing the consuming" (United Nations Development Programme et al. 2000, p. 23). Our desires to consume the basics and amenities of life affect the level of resources necessary to fulfill those demands, as well as the character of living landscapes that provide the sources and the sinks for those resources.

As noted, we live in *the first metropolitan century* with half of the world's population living in urban regions. In the future, even more people will move to cities. Global urban populations are expected to double by 2030 (United Nations Development Programme et al. 2000). By 2050, two-thirds of the people in the world will be living in urban regions. There are various estimates about trends in birth and life structure as well as the distribution of income and property, but all data suggest more people living in ever-expanding urban metropolitan regions.

Population changes – such as growth and migration – and consumption are related to urbanization and suburban sprawl. Halting, or at least managing, sprawl is an important issue for civic environmentalism (Dagger 2003) as well as for regional planning and community design. The movement of people to cities and metropolitan regions involves the transformation of spaces from rural, and natural to urban and suburban, the urbanization of the wild, the abandonment of the rural and the recovery of the core city and older suburban neighborhoods. Here are some key questions related to both population growth and urbanization:

- Why do people choose to live where they do?
- What policies direct/affect growth and development?
- What are the long-term impacts of these policies?
- What knowledge is necessary to inform interventions designed to mitigate those impacts?

Connectivity involves the ways that new networks and information systems will alter landscapes and communities, the transfer of knowledge, time, social relationships, and education. Connecting technologies – the automobile and the Internet – also may divide people and, thus, further fragment landscapes and communities. We constantly attempt to connect through information and transportation technologies. Connectivity will continue to transform human society, but how? Some queries we could use to find answers are the following:

- What will cities look like when people do not have to be next to each other for commercial reasons?
- How will business, educational, and public institutions be affected?
- How will connectivity affect use, knowledge, experience, and perception of our built environments?

Questions like these are being addressed by researchers in various disciplines. There is no lack of attention to the questions, but cohesiveness in providing the answers is missing.

Global environmental processes also drive landscape changes and adaptations. Climate change trends are well-known (Harrison and Pearce 2000). Increased carbon dioxide in the atmosphere is resulting in changes in rainfall, cloudiness, wind strength, and temperature. For example, these changes already influence the life cycles of polar bears in the Arctic; small islands are disappearing in the South Pacific as the calamities of nature increase; and the rain forest island habitats around mountaintops in Costa Rica are dwindling annually with less and less cloud cover to support moisture-dependent species.

In addition to global climate changes, local climates are changing as places undergo urbanization and suburbanization (Baker et al. 2002). Known as the "urban heat island" effect the change results as more surfaces are paved over. Black asphalt especially warms areas by absorbing and storing warmth. As we learn more about such drivers from the global to local scales, we can adjust our city and regional plans and community designs to mitigate deleterious consequences while taking strategic advantage of opportunities.

Land uses, land cover, and water resources are profoundly altered as urbanization trends proceed. In urbanizing regions of the United States, two of the most pressing land use and water related concerns have been, for many decades now, conversion of prime agricultural lands and degradation of water quality in surface streams, lakes, and aquifers. Local governmental policies relating to land use are the dominant means of managing densities and patterns of suburbanization, but they are either too lax or not applied over a sufficiently large regional area to adequately impede or control these trends.

Suburban sprawl consumes significant amounts of prime farmland in the United States. From the 1970s to the present, farmland conversion has been reported by various agencies. For example, according to the U.S. Department of Agriculture's National Resources Inventory, an average of 43 hectares of farmland was converted to non-agricultural use every hour each year between 1982 and 1992. In California's Central Valley region alone, 6,075 hectares of farmland are developed each year. That region produces 10 percent of the value of U.S. farm output on less than 1 percent of the nation's farmland (United States Department of Agriculture 2001). Roughly one-fifth of the nation's 101,250,000 hectares of prime agricultural land can be considered at risk for development because they are within 80.4 kilometers of the 100 largest cities in the nation (U.S. Secretary of Agriculture 2001).

These trends persist seemingly without impact on productivity or economic loss, as measured at the scale of the national economy. However, agricultural industries in metropolitan areas are steadily declining or vanishing. The definition and clarity of the rural-urban landscape fringe becomes muddled with low-density suburban sprawl or steady advances of new housing construction. An intricate and difficult set of problems ensues, whereby (1) farms become more valuable as substrate for future suburban housing projects; (2) farmers view their land and farm heritage as but a dying practice that will not be sustained in future generations; and (3) the land is readily acquirable and developable, even under restrictive local land use polices, because of the prevailing respect for individual property rights by local elected officials.

Similarly, water quality in urbanizing areas is subject to degradation by the slow, cumulative, area-wide effects of urban development and associated storm runoff pollution (Natural Resources Defense Council 2005). Area streams and lakes often are key elements of a region's landscape function and heritage. Yet, they generally undergo profound change as a result of highly erosive peak flow rates from impervious surfaces, sedimentation from land development and construction-stage surface erosion, and excessive nutrient and toxic chemical loading from residential lawns, automobile discharges, and urban-industrial spills. While point-source discharges of pollution into American rivers have been curtailed dramatically in the past 30 years, non-point sources such as urban runoff have only recently gotten the attention needed (Horner et al. 1994). Rivers and lakes in urbanizing areas of the United States typically are highly eutrophic and considerably more filled with sediment than in previous decades, and flow rates are much more extreme (lower base flows, higher peak flows). Demands for municipal water supplies also confound the water quality problems in urbanizing regions. Regional landscapes with highly prized surface waters are all too often faced with a dilemma – whether to encourage economic activity that stems from the pristine quality and attractiveness of the resource, or to regulate and limit those economic uses and activities so as to protect the resource.

How are we to respond to the challenges and opportunities presented by this change? Resiliency is one response strategy.

The Resilient Region

Resilience is a concept and a theory with growing appeal in the disciplines of ecology and planning. According to the ecologist Gunderson and his colleagues,

> *Resilience* has been defined in two different ways in the ecological literature, each reflecting different aspects of stability. One definition focuses on efficiency, constancy and predictability – all attributes of engineers' desire for fail-safe design. The other focuses on persistence, change and unpredictability – all attributes embraced and celebrated by evolutionary biologists and by those who search for safe-fail designs (Gunderson et al. 2002, p. 530).

The first definition is tied to standard ideas in ecology that emphasize equilibrium and stability. The second definition emerges from what is called "new ecology," which focuses on non-equilibrium and the adaptability of ecological systems (see, for example, Botkin 1990). Pickett and Cadenasso (2003) suggest that the latter is appropriate "to urban ecosystems, because it suggests that spatial heterogeneity is an important component of the persistence of adaptable metropolitan regions" (p. 34).

The application of resilience to urban ecosystems is largely of the result of the two National Science Foundation–funded urban long-term ecological research (LTER) projects in Phoenix and Baltimore (see www.caplter.asu.edu and www.beslter.org). Cities are anything but stable and predictable systems. The urban LTERs reinforce our growing appreciation for changing and adapting systems (see, for example, Musacchio and Wu 2004).

To a large degree, the interest from planners in resilience emerged post–September 11, 2001. The principal leaders of this interest are Lawrence Vale of the Massachusetts Institute of Technology and Thomas Campanella of the University of North Carolina (Vale and Campanella 2005a, 2005b). Although ecologists have speculated about the application of resilience to urban planning, up to this point there has been scant connection between the ecological and the planning resilience research.

Vale and Campanella link resilience with disasters, noting "Urban disaster, like urban resilience, takes many forms" (2005a, B6). Furthermore, they observe, "Many disasters may follow a predictable pattern of rescue, restoration, rebuilding, and remembrance, yet we can only truly evaluate a recovery based on special circumstances" (2005a, B6). Thus, urban resilience is linked to the specific qualities of the place where it occurs.

Vale and Campanella distinguish natural disasters from those caused by people. Natural disasters include those resulting from fire, earthquake, flood, drought, volcano, hurricane, tsunami, and epidemic disease. Human disasters result both from accidents and deliberate, place-targeted events (Vale and Campanella 2005b).

As a result of their study of disasters, Vale and Campanella present 12 axioms of resilience (Vale and Campanella 2005b):

1. Narratives of resilience are a political necessity.
2. Disasters reveal the resilience of governments.
3. Narratives of resilience are always contested.
4. Local resilience is linked to national renewal.
5. Resilience is underwritten by outsiders.
6. Urban rebuilding symbolizes human resilience.
7. Remembrance drives resilience.
8. Resilience benefits from inertia of prior investment.
9. Resilience exploits the power of place.
10. Resilience casts opportunism as opportunity.
11. Resilience, like disaster, is site-specific.
12. Resilience entails more than rebuilding.

As they acknowledge, Vale and Campanella build their axioms on the considerable body of work done by American planners on the topic of disaster. One of the few times the American public turns to planners is in the wake of tragedy. Might not resilience also be a helpful concept for guiding metropolitan regions in times without disaster?

Such regional resilience would be based on enhancing social capital, creating knowledge capital, and protecting natural capital. How might universities assist in advancing such regional resilience? Examples from Phoenix and Austin offer some suggestions.

Greater Phoenix 2100

The Sun Belt grew at spectacular rates in the late 20th century, and among western U.S. cities, Phoenix and its metropolitan region led the pack. The United States Census Bureau reports that between 1990 and 2000, Maricopa County was the fastest-growing county in the nation at 44.8 percent, increasing from 2,122,101 to 3,072,149 people. The county is the fourth largest in the nation in total population. During the 1990s, the city of Phoenix topped one million people and became the sixth largest U.S. city. Its spatial expanse has eclipsed that of the city of Los Angeles. According to the city's Planning Department data, the region is growing by about 63,000 residents per year and requires about 23,000 new housing units to meet the demand. Statewide, the population is growing by more than 2,000 residents per week, and the number of people in the state is expected to double in the next 20 years.

The weather, relatively affordable housing, and abundant jobs attract a diverse array of newcomers, but increased population has numerous social and environmental consequences. Debate rages about the impacts of growth locally and nationally: Is it good? Is it deleterious? Can it be sustained? At what cost? Who benefits? Who suffers?

In 2000, a group of Arizona State University (ASU) faculty recognized that these phenomena represent an opportunity for both research and public service in this fast-growing urban environmental laboratory. Furthermore, knowledge gleaned from such inquiries could lead to smarter growth and more livable places in the future. This notion provides the intellectual foundation for a project named Greater Phoenix 2100 (GP 2100), which seeks to provide data and analysis to the region's decision makers to help them make wise choices about the future (Fink et al. 2003).

GP 2100 built on two ongoing ASU activities. The first was the North Area studies that involved faculty from the College of Architecture and Environmental Design in planning a 135-square mile area in Phoenix (Steiner 2000). The second was the Central Arizona/Phoenix (CAP) LTER (see Collins et al. 2000). GP 2100 combined the scientific approach of the LTER with the planning activities of the North Area work.

With the support of the Lincoln Institute of Land Policy, the GP 2100 leadership team organized a workshop in April 2001 to help chart the course for the project. Daniel B. Botkin of the University of California-Santa Barbara, Michael Crow of Columbia University, Helen Ingram of the University of California-Irvine, and Robert Yaro of the Regional Plan Association formed a panel of outside experts. As a result of the workshop, it was determined that ASU should create various scenarios for the future in a "Sim Phoenix" format and a "Decision Theater" that would be a physical and a virtual place where academic and community leaders could probe the consequences of possible actions.

Databases and Audiences

Still in its early stages, ASU's GP 2100 seeks to coordinate federal, state, and academic information programs relating to the environment of the region. The project will be linked with similar studies in other metropolitan areas and global city regions (Simmonds and Hack 2000). GP 2100 will answer questions that people care about by providing objective, scientifically based information using state-of-the-art forecasting and decision tools and theories. Coupled with the CAP LTER, GP 2100 has the potential to launch a network of similar undertakings nationally and internationally.

GP 2100 will develop and present a wide variety of scientific and technical data on the past, present, and possible futures of the Phoenix metropolitan region. The project builds on the premise that knowledge can be used to create better lives for future generations. GP 2100 will provide learning and research experiences to six major groups of people:

1. Regional decision makers and community leaders. Many activities, including community visioning exercises and open-space ballot initiatives, point to an acute need for regional leadership. Regional decision makers have identified the need for sound, long-term environmental information.
2. The general public. GP 2100 will generate considerable interest within the metropolitan Phoenix community. According to several opinion polls, the public is deeply concerned about growth, environmental quality, and the livability of their neighborhoods.
3. Middle- and high-school students and teachers. The project will offer engaging learning opportunities for students and teachers about scientific and decision-making processes. The multi-scale aspect of the project will enable teachers to illustrate how specific neighborhoods are connected to regional systems.
4. ASU faculty. GP 2100 will be an umbrella and a catalyst for researchers studying the urban ecologies of the region. It will provide the opportunity to explore the integration of scientific information, the examination of new technologies for representation and visualization, and a platform for advancing modeling and decision theory.
5. ASU students. Both undergraduate and graduate students will be engaged in GP 2100's unique multidisciplinary studies that will contribute to an improved quality of life in the region.
6. Future generations. The century-long approach means that there will be several generations of audiences.

Goals and Benefits

GP 2100's goal is to make the best possible scientific and technical information available in ways that will enable wise, knowledge-based decision-making that can shape the region during the next 100 years. This timeframe presents a purposefully longer-term view of the metropolitan region than has previously been developed. While short-term visioning is limited by immediate considerations, a century-long perspective requires the incorporation of multigenerational concerns and changes in technology. A 100-year timeframe also allows for evaluation of impacts of such geologically common events as droughts, major floods, and gradual climate changes. In short, GP 2100 will be a strong scientific resource for considering the region's long-term prospects and creating the kind of future its residents want.

Two types of benefits will flow from the project. The first relates to the future quality of life in the region. An underlying assumption of GP 2100 is that better information will lead to wiser decision making that will, in turn, result in healthier, more livable communities. Metropolitan Phoenix is expected to double from 3 to 6 million people in the next 20 or 30 years. Meanwhile, global populations will grow and become more urban. Such growth poses many challenges relating to land use, transportation, open space, biodiversity, urban design, recreation, employment, equity, air quality, water quality and quantity, and the overall quality of life of city regions. The GP 2100 effort will be beneficial to those who are addressing these concerns in Phoenix by providing a prototype of how science-based tools and a regional perspective can better inform long-term decision making. By viewing the Phoenix region as an urban environmental laboratory, the lessons learned will have implications for the broader scientific and policy communities.

GP 2100 also will be an asset for ASU researchers and students, who will have the opportunity to collaborate in multidisciplinary teams and will have access to state-of-the-art geographic information systems (GIS) and visualization technologies. New and emerging theories in urban and landscape ecology, decision science, land use and environmental modeling, and biocomplexity will be explored.

Special Features

Several linked products are envisioned to flow from GP 2100. Existing data can be coalesced into a dynamic warehouse of continuously updated regional information. The concept was that such a data repository can be presented to the public through an Urban eAtlas, which could be made available in electronic and more conventional forms to provide documentation of existing conditions and enable the construction of future scenarios. The digital version will be available online so it may be continuously accessed and updated. The paper version of the atlas became the first product of GP 2100 and was published in 2003 (Quay 2003).

The data archives and Urban eAtlas will contribute to a third major product: Sim Phoenix, an interactive computer game that can help researchers, citizens, and decision makers visualize the consequences of "what if" scenarios. Sim Phoenix is a step toward the creation of an even more ambitious visualization project: a Decision Theater where local leaders, citizens, students, and researchers can explore future options for the region. The Decision Theater will be a physical space in which scientific data, group dynamics, and interactive computer technology are used to develop simulations of the region's futures and considerations of their consequences. The simulations and their representations will evolve with new computational and representational technologies as well as with new scientific information.

GP 2100 will complement and augment existing long-term monitoring activities being conducted at ASU, such as the CAP LTER project, one of only two such urban LTER sites in the nation. Launching a satellite in cooperation with NASA is one monitoring possibility. This "Phoenix-Sat" would pass over the region twice daily, enabling diurnal measurements of such dynamic parameters as traffic, air quality, soil moisture, and construction. It is possible that the Phoenix-Sat could be part of a larger international remote-sensing program for urban resource monitoring. Tools such as the data archives, Urban eAtlas, Sim Phoenix, the Decision Theater, and Phoenix-Sat will enable scholars and decision makers alike to probe the major issues that metropolitan areas like Phoenix will face in the coming century. As a result, problems may be foreseen and avoided and opportunities pursued with vigor.

ASU faculty in the life, physical, and social sciences are compiling a comprehensive suite of information about the region. Planners, policy analysts, and educators also could identify a series of key response variables and parameters for a Decision Theater. Computer scientists could program this complex information so that it can be displayed in both two- and three-dimensional formats, as well as animated views illustrating changes through time. The data could be automatically updated from dynamic government and university databases, from hundreds of sensors throughout the metropolitan region, and from orbiting satellites.

In this first-of-its-kind Decision Theater, high-quality audio and visual presentation systems will include a 270-degree screen, which provides an immersive, synthetic environment along with comfortable ergonomics. This arrangement enables decision makers and researchers to come together to explore, debate, and analyze options for the future. The Decision Theater is capable of high-resolution stereoscopic viewing using shuttered glasses. A visitor can have her or his viewing position tracked ("head-tracking"), giving the impression of truly walking within the data and data results, pondering the possible landscapes of the future from different angles. It could be associated with an innovative Planetary Imaging Faculty set up jointly by ASU and the Jet Propulsion Laboratory, as well as dance and visual representation projects from ASU's Institute for Studies in the Arts. While real-time interaction with data and models in the Decision Theater is engrossing, a comparably rich online experience also is possible through the use of Web-based multimedia, text, data download and upload, and modeling tools. The virtual Decision Theater allows a participant to interact with a Sim Phoenix–like game.

How will the Decision Theater be implemented? Four interactive parameters appear especially crucial for modeling the future: water availability, air quality, open space, and land use. ASU and its community and government partners already possess an enormous storehouse of data on these parameters, but the challenge is to combine the data in meaningful ways. To this end, the Greater Phoenix 2100 team, in conjunction with the Arizona Department of Water Resources and the U.S. Geological Survey, now is developing a water availability prototype that would use the hydrologic cycle to model regional water availability using factors of precipitation, supply, evaporation, and demand to illustrate water futures both graphically and spatially.

Progress Report

Since it began in 2000, what progress has been achieved beyond the urban atlas? One of the outside experts for the Lincoln-sponsored workshop, Michael Crow, became president of ASU. Since then, he has provided steadfast support for GP 2100. In 2003, ASU organized a Consortium for the Study of Rapidly Urbanizing Regions. The consortium is one of Michael Crows "use-inspired" research initiatives developed to apply fundamental research to community, national, and global problems. In support of these initiatives, philanthropist Julie Ann Wrigley gave ASU a $15 million gift to establish an International Institute for Sustainability to address regional and global environmental threats. At about the same time, ASU received a $6.9 million National Science Foundation grant to establish the Decision Center for a Desert City. Following this grant, Ira A. Fulton, a prominent Phoenix businessman, made a gift of $3 million to establish a Decision Theater for a New Arizona.

The ideas launched by the GP 2100 team are receiving significant support and have helped to frame ASU's research and outreach agenda.

Envision Central Texas

As Richard Dagger notes, "Campaigns to curb urban sprawl have met with firm and well-financed opposition" (2003, p. 29). As a result, an example of a campaign to positively manage growth, that was both well-financed and strongly supported, might provide a welcome antidote. The Envision Central Texas project is an example of regional planning and visioning. It may also be viewed as an application of human ecology with implications of design for civic environmentalism with the University of Texas at Austin playing a central role.

Austin has a history of experimentation with innovative planning endeavors from "Austin Tomorrow" in the 1970s through "negotiated growth management" in the 1980s on to "Smart Growth" in the 1990s, with mixed implementation results along the way (for example, see Butler and Myers 1984). On the positive side, the Lake Austin plan, known locally as the "McHarg Plan," pioneered water quality planning in the 1970s (Wallace McHarg Roberts and Todd 1976). More recently, the Balcones Canyonlands Conservation program was widely heralded for its innovation in habitat conservation planning (see Beatley 1994). However, other efforts have experienced less success. The city's Save Our Springs Ordinance, limiting impervious surfaces over the aquifer recharge zone, was circumvented by developers who had the ordinance weakened by the state. Past efforts have tended to focus on Austin, ignoring the larger region. Envision Central Texas differs because of the involvement of five counties and many smaller cities in addition to Austin. At the very least, Envision Central Texas prompted local citizens to begin thinking regionally.

The Austin metropolitan region – defined by the central city and the five surrounding counties (Bastrop, Caldwell, Hays, Travis, and Williamson), has a population greater than 1.25 million people. The metropolitan region grew by 47 percent in the decade of 1990–2000, and is projected to attain 2.75–3.0 million people by 2030 (Capital Area Metropolitan Planning Organization 2005). The five-county region covers 11,000 square kilometers (km), of which approximately 3,000 square km is developed. Regionally, the population density is very low – only 113 persons/square km and is expected to double in the next 20 to 30 years. By comparison, this region is approximately one-third the size of the Netherlands and only one-fourth as dense (33,883 square km, 477 persons/square km) (United States Central Intelligence Agency 2003). Astonishingly, the region lacks a growth plan. In response, local civic leaders launched Envision Central Texas (ECT). The effort is a private, nonprofit organization, not a government agency, although it receives funding from several local governments. Its board retained the planning and architecture firm Fregonese Calthorpe Associates as consultants. John Fregonese is the former planning director of Portland Metro in Oregon. Peter Calthorpe is a leading New Urbanist architect (Calthorpe 1993; Calthorpe and Fulton 2001). Fregonese Calthorpe Associates and the ECT board sought to create a vision uniting the Austin metropolitan region around common strategies, resolving disputes, and addressing critical issues.

To accomplish these objectives, an extensive public process was organized that involved workshops where hundreds of participants built their own growth scenarios of the Central Texas region. Fregonese Calthorpe Associates then digitized the maps through GIS (building on a GIS database created by the University of Texas at Austin School of Architecture). Scenario planning, a tool for assessing the consequences for development and conservation in an uncertain world, was the theoretical basis for the process (Peterson, Cumming, and Carpenter 2003; Peterson et al. 2003). Scenario planning is "a systemic method for thinking creatively about possible complex and uncertain futures" (Peterson, Cumming, and Carpenter 2003, p. 359). Scenarios are "plausible stories of what might unfold in the future" (Mulvihill 2003, p. 45). Fregonese distinguished this type of planning from traditional planning because the result was a vision, or a series of visions, rather than a plan.

Scenarios for Central Texas

Four scenarios resulted from the ECT process, using available land to direct future land use and transportation systems in different patterns and arrangements. Economic, land use, and transportation models were used for this stage. Existing conditions and trends, such as current and planned transportation corridors, were considered. Similarly, critical natural resources such as aquifer recharge zones and productive agricultural lands were taken into account during the visioning process. The four scenarios were formulated to reveal classical differences in growth policies and resultant development patterns, based on citizen guidance and expressed opinions at the regional workshops.

Scenario A is the "business-as-usual" projection. This scheme spreads another 1.25 million people across the landscape in patterns similar to recent developments, using transportation systems already approved. Most residents would live in single-family houses built on previously undeveloped land, and most jobs would be located in the central city. As a result, people would continue to commute to work by car. The next 1.25 million people would live on 1,900 square km of additional land at a density of 660 persons/square km.

In Scenario B, most new growth would surround major roadways, both new and existing. Housing and job growth would occur throughout the five counties. Some redevelopment would occur in existing neighborhoods. Overall, most residents would still live in single-family houses. Regional transportation options would include toll roads, new express bus routes, a commuter rail system, and a central light-rail system. The next 1.25 million people would live on approximately 800 square km of additional land at a density of more than 1,500 persons/square km.

With Scenario C, growth would occur in both existing communities and emerging new towns. Current towns and cities would gain jobs and residents, but even more mixed-use development would result in fewer residents in single-family houses. New towns would be built along major roads and railways, preserving open space and undeveloped land between communities. The next 1.25 million people would live on approximately 725 square km of additional land at a density of more than 1,700 persons/square km.

In Scenario D, most growth would occur in existing towns and communities. More land would remain undeveloped than in other scenarios, with about one-third of new households and two-thirds of new jobs located on currently developed land. Regional transportation options would include toll roads, extensive commuter rail, light rail, and express bus lines. The next 1.25 million people would live on approximately 385 square km of additional land at a density of more than 3,200 persons/square km.

The four scenarios were analyzed for planning consequences relating to land development, agricultural and range land conversion, new development over the aquifers, annual weekly travel time per person, housing options (e.g., single family vs. multifamily), infrastructure costs for new development, and regional transportation options. Indicators were established for each of these impacts so citizens, elected officials, and planners could compare the consequences of pursuing each scenario. In addition to the regional scenarios, Fregonese Calthorpe developed site-specific designs for six actual places in the region. These designs helped residents to visualize different possible future community developments (Calthorpe Associates 2003).

Austin 1951 compared with Austin 2002

In October 2003, the four scenarios were presented to the public in an extensive public participation process. Surveys were distributed in all the local newspapers and made available on the Internet, and more than 12,000 were returned. The purpose of the regionwide survey was to assess public preferences for the scenarios and the consequences. The results were analyzed and a draft consensus vision brought back to the community in early 2004. Clearly the most highly favored scenario throughout the region was Scenario D, in which most new growth would occur in existing towns and built-up areas (see Table 1).

Following the survey, a consensus scenario was developed and distributed in May 2004 (Envision Central Texas 2004) (see also www.envisioncentraltexas.org). The vision report presented four strategic roles for Envision Central Texas (Envision Central Texas 2004):

1. Demonstrate and model positive examples of increased density and mixed use that have been achieved by public-private partnerships in concert with local planning processes.
2. Analyze the best practices in the United States in creating a regional open-space funding plan that provides fair compensation to landowners.
3. Assist communities to develop goals that will close the gap for the underprivileged and underserved populations, particularly in the areas of health, education, housing, jobs, and transportation.
4. Recognize projects and initiatives that demonstrate best practices for achieving the regional vision.

Progress Report

To pursue these strategic roles, seven implementation committees were organized: transportation and land-use integration, economic development coordination, housing and jobs balance, density and mixed use, open space funding, social equity, and best practices recognition. The committees began their work in the late summer into the early fall of 2004. For example, in October 2004, the transportation and land-use

Table 1. Results of Citizen Survey

Percent of 12,000 responses voting in favor of Scenario D

Best use of land	57%
Best use of agricultural land	55%
Best to serve future transportation needs	67%
Best to serve overall quality of life	47%

integration committee organized a transit oriented development (TOD) symposium at the University of Texas. The TOD symposium included national and local leaders and was held in advance of an election by Austin voters on a commuter rail initiative. The TOD symposium was well attended, and the November 2004 commuter rail vote was overwhelmingly positive.

In January 2005, the mayor of Austin proposed an "Envision Central Texas" bond election. The mayor's goal was to implement the Envision Central Texas vision by funding open space acquisition and inner-city infrastructure improvement. Furthermore, an Austin city councilman with the city's planning department proposed a complete overhaul of commercial development design guidelines, again to further the vision. Implementing the Envision Central Texas vision is seen as an iterative, ongoing effort.

The University of Texas at Austin is a partner in the ECT process. University faculty and administrators have been active on committees and at workshops in both participatory and leadership capacities. Faculty and students have provided GIS services and data. ECT has been the subject of research and design studio projects. The university has contributed funding to ECT and as the iterative effort continues, will continue to play an important role, especially through the School of Architecture and the Center for Sustainable Development.

Models for Other Metropolitan Regions

Generations of citizens and scholars will benefit from Greater Phoenix 2100 and Envision Central Texas. The projects will result in products to help community and business leaders make wiser decisions. They will assist local, state, and federal officials in planning and designing programs and policies. Greater Phoenix 2100 will aid teachers and students in their understanding of natural and social processes. The project presents uniquely complex targets for technological, scientific and policy analysis advancements. It will produce and facilitate interaction with massive, typically disparate, datasets. Because its major components are easily transferable to other urban regions, the project can provide a model for other places interested in pursuing similar initiatives. In this century, some two-thirds of the world's population will live in urban areas. Both Envision Central Texas and Greater Phoenix 2100 have far-reaching implications concerning the application of knowledge capital to regional and urban decision making to maximize social capital while maintaining the natural capital of the metropolitan region.

Acknowledgments

The Greater Phoenix 2100 section was based on and updated an article in *Land Lines* (Steiner 2001). The Envision Central Texas section evolved from two papers by Steiner and Kent Butler (Steiner and Butler 2004, 2005). The support of the Lincoln Institute for Land Policy and the collaboration with Kent Butler are much appreciated.

References

Baker, L., A. J. Brazel, N. Selover, C. Martin, N. McIntyre, F. R. Steiner, A. Nelson, and L. Musacchio. 2002. Urbanization and Warming of Phoenix (Arizona, USA): Impacts, Feedbacks, and Mitigation. *Urban Ecosystems* 6 (3): 188–203.

Barrett, Gary W. and Eugene P. Odum. 2000. The Twenty-First Century: The World at Carrying-Capacity. *Bio Science* 50 (4): 363–368.

Beatley, Timothy. 1994. *Habitat Conservation Planning*. Austin, TX: University of Texas Press.

Botkin, Daniel B. 1990. *Discordant Harmonies: A New Ecology for the Twenty-First Century*. New York: Oxford University Press.
Brand, Stewart. 1999. *The Clock of the Long Now*. New York: Basic Books.

Butler, Kent and Dowell Myers. 1984. Boomtown in Austin, Texas: Negotiated Growth Management. *Journal of the American Planning Association* 50(4): 447–458.

Calthorpe Associates. 2003. Proposed Urban Design Guidelines, East Austin Rail Corridor, Featherlite, Austin, Texas. Austin, TX: Envision Central Texas.

Calthorpe, Peter. 1993. *The Next American Metropolis: Ecology, Community, and the American Dream*. New York: Princeton Architectural Press.
Calthorpe, Peter and William Fulton. 2001. *The Regional City: Planning for the End of Sprawl*. Washington, DC: Island Press.

Capital Area Metropolitan Planning Organization. 2005. Unpublished data presenting area population growth, 2003 and 2030. Austin, TX: Author.

Collins, James R., Ann Kinzig, Nancy B. Grimm, William F. Fagan, Diane Hope, Jiango Wu, and Elizabeth T. Borer. 2000. A New Urban Ecology. *American Scientist* 8(5): 416–425.

Dagger, Richard. 2003. Stopping Sprawl for the Good of All: The Case for Civic Environmentalism. *Journal of Social Philosophy* 34 (1): 28–43.

Envision Central Texas. 2004. *A Vision for Central Texas*. Austin, Texas.

Fink, Jonathan, Frederick Steiner, Nancy B. Grimm, and Charles L. Redman. 2003. Greater Phoenix 2100: Building a National Urban Environmental Research Agenda. In *Earth Sciences in the City: A Reader*, Grant Heiken, Robert Fakundiny, John Sutter (eds.), pp. 413–416. Washington, DC: American Geophysical Union.

Gunderson, Lance, C. S. Holling, L. Pritchard, and G. D. Peterson. 2002. Resilience. In

Encyclopedia of Global Environmental Change, Ted Munn (ed.), pp. 530–531.

Harrison, Paul and Fred Pearce. 2000. *AAA Atlas of Population and Environment*. Berkeley, CA: University of California Press.

Horner, R. R., J. J. Skupien, E. H. Livingston, and H. E. Shaver. 1994. *Fundamentals of Urban Runoff Management: Technical and Institutional Issues*. Washington, DC: Terrene Institute.

Mulvahill, Peter R. 2003. Expanding the Scoping Community. *Environmental Impact Assessment Review* 23:39–49.

Musacchio, Laura and Jianguo Wu, invited guest editors. 2004. Collaborative Research in Landscape-Scale Ecosystem Studies: Emerging Trends in Urban and Regional Ecology. *Urban Ecosystems* 7(3): 175–314.
Natural Resources Defense Council. 2005. *Urban Stormwater Pollution—Fact and Fiction*. Online reference: www.nrdc.org/water/pollution/q2storm.asp.

Peterson, Garry D., Graeme S. Cumming, and Stephen R. Carpenter. 2003. Scenario Planning: A Tool for Conservation in an Uncertain World. *Conservation Biology* 17(2). 358–366.

Peterson, Garry D., T. Douglas Beard Jr., Beatrix E. Beisner, Elena M. Bennett, Stephen R. Carpenter, Graeme S. Cumming, C. Lisa Dent, and Tanya D. Havlicek. 2003. Assessing Future Ecosystem Services: A Case Study of the Northern Highlands Lake District, Wisconsin. *Conservation Ecology* 7(3): 1–19.

Pickett, Steward T. A. and Mary L. Cadenasso. 2003. Integrating the Ecological, Socioeconomic, and Planning Realms: Insights from the Baltimore Ecosystem Study. In Pattern, Process, Scale, and Hierarchy: Advancing Interdisciplinary Collaboration for Creating Sustainable Urban Landscapes and Communities, Laura Musacchio, Jianguo Wu, and Thara Johnson (eds.), p. 34. Tempe, AZ: Arizona State University.

Quay, Ray (ed.). 2003. *Greater Phoenix Regional Atlas: A Preview of the Region's 50-Year Future*. Tempe, AZ: Greater Phoenix 2100, Arizona State University.

Simmonds, Roger and Gary Hack (eds.). 2000. *Global City Regions: Their Emerging Forms*. London: Spon Press.

Steiner, Frederick. 2000. *The Living Landscape* (second edition). New York: McGraw-Hill.

Steiner, Frederick. 2001. Greater Phoenix 2100: Knowledge Capital, Social Capital, Natural Capital. *Land Lines* 13 (5, September): 1–3, 14.

Steiner, Frederick and Kent Butler. 2004. The Green Heart of Texas. Multiple Landscape, Merging Past and Present in Landscape Planning. The Netherlands: Wageningen University.

Steiner, Frederick and Kent Butler. 2005. The Green Heart of Texas: Water and Scenario Planning in the Austin Region. Paesaggi Fluviali Agricoltura e Citta Convergna, Polytechnic of Turin, Italy.

United Nations, 1998. *World Population Prospects: The 1996 Revisions*. New York: The United Nations.

United Nations Development Programme, United Nations Environment Program, World Bank, World Resources Institute. 2000. *World Resources 2000-2001, People and Ecosystems, The Fraying Web of Life*. Amsterdam: Elsevier.

United States Department of Agriculture. 2001. *Census of Agriculture 1997*. Washington: U.S. Department of Agriculture.

United States Central Intelligence Agency. 2003. *The World Fact Book 2003*. Online: www.cia.gov/cia/publications/factbook/.

Vale, Lawrence J. and Thomas J. Campanella. 2005a. The City Shall Rise Again: Urban Resilience in the Wake of Disaster. *The Chronicle of Higher Education*, January 14: B6–B9.

Vale, Lawrence J. and Thomas J. Campanella. 2005b. *The Resilient City: How Modern Cities Recover from Disaster*. New York: Oxford University Press.

Wallace McHarg Roberts and Todd. 1976. *Lake Austin Growth Management Plan*. Austin: City of Austin.

Chapter 2
Education and Transformation

David W. Orr

The challenge presented to us is to imagine "how graduate education and research may lead to the transformation of major metropolitan areas." This is a bold challenge for several reasons, not the least of which is that educational institutions have more often followed, not led, economic trends and urban settlement patterns. Second, it presumes that an educational enterprise can surmount other trends and "drivers" by the power of ideas and educational vendors to substantially improve the surrounding urban prospect. This essay begins by describing four factors that will affect this effort, and concludes with thoughts about what a dynamic university might do relative to those challenges and the charge to lead in the transformation of the metropolitan Washington region.

Forces and Drivers

1. Climate/Energy

In the early years of the 21st century, it is clear that human demands of a rising population and expanding global economy will have to be recalibrated to match ecological capacities. The exploitation of natural capital, characteristic of the industrial age, must necessarily and fairly quickly give way to a global economy that preserves soils, forests, climate resilience, and biological diversity. The most urgent task ahead will be to stabilize and then reduce greenhouse gases, of which carbon dioxide (CO_2) is the most important.

The risks of climate destabilization ahead have been described by Watson et al. (2001) and are substantial. The scientists of the IPCC forecast temperature increases in this century ranging from 2.5 F to 10.4 F. More recent studies published in Powslon (2005) suggest that the warming may, in fact, be twice as high (5-20 F), and that a 2 C rise above the pre-industrial level may be the threshold for runaway climate destabilization (we are at ~ .7 C). At some point in that range, all hell breaks loose and all bets are off. The Millennium Ecosystem Assessment (2005) documents other changes in global biogeochemical cycles that pose serious challenges ahead, including a rapid increase in Nitrogen flowing into ecosystems causing biological havoc. The multiple challenges ahead, summarized in the term "sustainability," have to do with policies, institutional innovations, and behavioral changes have the effects of removing carbon fuels from the energy system, reducing much of the material flows inherent in the extractive economy, and adopting methods of pricing and valuation that honor the well-being of those seven generations hence.

That part of the transition specifically related to the energy system is the key to the transition to sustainability. A considerable amount of attention has recently been given to the subject of "peak oil extraction " and the work of Campbell (2004) and Deffeyes (2003). Estimates of the year of global peak oil extraction vary by about three decades. Deffeyes believes that the peak will occur in late 2005 or early 2006. Everyone agrees, however, that the end of the era of cheap oil is in sight. Signs of an impending peak in recent months include the drop of 40 percent in reserve estimates by Shell Oil, declining pressure in some Saudi oil fields, and statements by OPEC officials that they are already at capacity. The transition when it occurs will be made more difficult by the lack of any coherent energy transition strategy by the United States, the largest consumer of fossil energy and emitter of greenhouse gases.

But the course of wise policy is clear, beginning with the transition from a fossil fuel powered global civilization to a much more efficient energy regime (four to ten times more efficient) powered by solar energy in its various forms and perhaps hydrogen (not a source of energy, but a carrier). The benefits of doing so are equally clear and offer ramifying benefits:

- Reduce or eliminate oil imports
- Reduce dependence on Middle Eastern oil
- Lessen our military engagement in an unstable region
- Cut our balance of payments deficit
- Lower the cost of energy in the economy
- Create millions of new jobs
- Minimize oil spills and water pollution
- Reduce land degradation by strip-mining
- Reduce air pollution
- Improve health
- Lower medical expenses
- Remove influence of fossil energy companies on U.S. politics
- Improve the health of our democracy
- Contribute to stabilizing climate
- Enable us to avoid a catastrophe
- Improve our reputation and standing in the community of nations

Each of these collateral benefits of efficiency and renewable energy is well known and well documented. Opinion polls show that the public across the entire political spectrum is ready for the transition to a smarter energy policy based on efficiency and solar energy.

2. The Bush Legacy

The legacy of the George W. Bush administration bears heavily on the issues being discussed. The Bush administration is attempting to eliminate funding, such as it is, for many urban programs and Amtrak. Long neglected, urban areas will be under increased financial stress. Perhaps the largest change, however, is the concentration of political power in the right wing of a single political party—James Madison's nightmare (*Federalist Papers* #10). But it is more sweeping than Madison feared it could be. In addition to controlling the Presidency, both houses of Congress, and the Supreme Court, the right wing of the Republican Party also controls most regulatory agencies, the intelligence community, much of the federal court system, substantial parts of the press, a majority of state houses, and reportedly is aiming its sights on educational institutions.

The war against terrorism is being used as leverage domestically in a "cultural war" and to quell opposition for many decades to come. Long before September 11, 2001, Newt Gingrich, the chief architect of the "Contract with America," said that it would be misleading to call these changes conservative, for the intent is a revolutionary change in American society toward an unfettered and concentrated, but highly subsidized, market.

3. Capabilities: Technological and Analytical

The intellectual capital and know-how necessary to create a sustainable society has expanded markedly since the first Earth Day in 1970. The revolution in ecological design is being driven by better technology, improved analytical abilities, and a growing comprehension of natural processes as a basis for human systems. The emergence of the U.S. Green Building Council and green architecture is one of the great success stories of the past three decades. It is estimated that about 6 percent of all commercial buildings now in planning or construction will be LEED certified. Data from a growing body of experience shows that high performance buildings can be built at or even below the cost of conventional structures, while reducing costs for energy, water, and maintenance, and improving occupant's satisfaction and productivity.

There also is a revolution in energy technologies evident in the declining cost and increasing performance of photovoltaics, wind, and fuel cell technologies. The upshot is the potential to create distributed energy systems based on small-scale, robust, portable, relatively inexpensive, easily maintained, networked, and resilient technologies with few environmental impacts while being implausible targets for terrorists.

In fields such as industrial ecology and biomimicry, other possibilities are emerging, including those to eliminate pollution by clustering businesses so that the wastes of one become the feedstock of another. Biomimicry represents a more thoroughgoing revolution based on the application of 3.8 billion years of evolutionary experience to manufacturing, fuel production, and materials (Benyus 2002). Applied to agriculture, for example, the scientific basis for using natural systems as a model for farming is coming on the horizon. Even more accepted forms of organic agriculture are growing from a small base, but at more than 25 percent per year. Other parts of an ecological design revolution include ecological engineering for wastewater treatment, ecological landscaping, and ecological restoration. Impressive as isolated components, the real power of ecological design is in the combination of technologies and practices in larger systems having substantial synergies and economic multipliers leading toward sustainable regional economies.

Making a solid and visually compelling case for sustainability will require better analytical tools that highlight full costs at a wider scale over longer time periods. Typical accounting and much of neoclassical economics is premised on the idea that costs ought to be narrowly assigned, and those not easily quantified can be imposed on others somewhere else or at some later time. The result is an economy that pushes its acknowledged and unacknowledged debt forward like a bow wave in front of a ship. New analytical tools, however, such as GIS analysis and remote sensing, permit a finer assessment of costs to landscapes, waters, and vegetation. Footprint analysis, developed by Rees and Wackernagel (1995), facilitates assessment of ecological costs as a footprint of land required for food production, carbon sequestration or energy production, waste cycling, and material production. Ecological economics, similarly, permits a finer grained assessment of true costs.

4. The Transformation of Higher Education

Higher education is being transformed by a variety of forces including rising costs, diminished government support, the ongoing revolution in information technology, and demographics. Relative to the cost of living, the cost of a four-year liberal arts education has soared due to rising expenses for research, laboratory, and computer equipment per faculty. It is likely that such costs will continue to rise for the foreseeable future. At the same time, the information revolution is increasing the capability of competitors such as the Internet-based University of Phoenix and other less conventional vendors, including nonprofit organizations that offer specialized instruction. The monopoly on information once held by colleges and universities has been broken by the Internet. One of the remaining values of conventional baccalaureate or graduate degree is the cash value of the degree itself. But that advantage also is likely to be challenged in coming years.

To stay competitive, conventional colleges and universities will have to be highly innovative about curriculum, pedagogy, and what might otherwise be called product development and marketing. Their position is not unlike that of, say, General Motors and Ford circa 1970 confronting competition from companies such as Toyota and Honda. Having lost their one-time position of dominance of the world market, their very survival is now uncertain. That sad story should be regarded as a cautionary tale for the leaders in higher education. The technological capability and know-how to establish a more resilient economy on distributed, locally available energy systems is at the core of a design revolution that is gathering steam. In this context educational institutions that are agile, creative, and visionary can make a very substantial difference within their region and beyond.

Transformation

> *What is the role of graduate education, research, and outreach in guiding the forthcoming transformation in ways that improve humankind? In particular, how can Virginia Tech's graduate programs in design, natural resource planning, policy, and science/technology studies in metropolitan Washington, DC, assume leadership to facilitate this transformation?*

The question itself might form the core of a unique curriculum in which the institution measures its performance relative to indicators of regional sustainability developed and monitored by students and faculty across a variety of disciplines. To reach that point, however, it would be necessary to define what is meant by "transformation" and "improve humankind" in order to clarify the vision brought to this effort. There is no doubt that the Washington, DC, metropolitan region will be transformed. Trends well underway are moving it toward a future of greater sprawl, more congestion, and more pollution typical of megapolitan growth in the past century. Even in the space of 14 years, the metropolitan region has sprawled considerably. (Figure 1)

But neither the vision nor the governmental capacity exists at the moment to implement an alternative and better future for the region. There are, however, examples around the world of city/regions that have addressed issues of sustainability with some success,

Figure 1. Settlement Patterns for an Alternative Future for the Washington, DC, Region

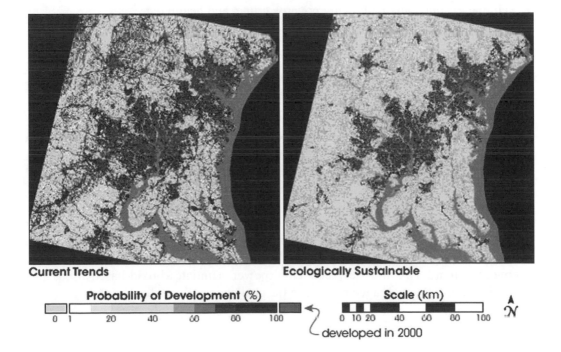

including Portland, OR; Seattle, WA; and Curitiba, Brazil. Discussions about smart growth and sustainability are under way in hundreds of cities and towns throughout the United States, but with a few notable exceptions, they have not been driven by an educational institution.

What would it mean to adopt the transformation of the metropolitan region as the core mission for the Virginia Tech campus in the capital region? Six key steps should be taken.

The first step is adapting the curriculum. The idea of using the region as the core of a curriculum goes back at least to the writings of John Dewey and Lewis Mumford, the regional planning movement of the 1930s, and in the global discussion about sustainability. More recently it is the core of by Rees and Wackernagel (1995) methodology for ecological footprinting and work in Austin and Phoenix described in Frederick Steiner's paper.

Transformed into curriculum and research, regional analysis would begin by acquiring baseline data about the region including:

- Ecological data, e.g., soils, rainfall, topography, ecology, geology, settlement patterns, air and water quality, toxic pollution, etc.
- Detailed information on spatial distribution and trends (such as those illustrated in Figure 1)
- Resource flow analysis showing the footprint and quantity of energy and goods, including electricity, fuels, materials, and food, that enter the metropolitan area and that leave it as waste
- Human resource maps showing poverty, crime, and health data
- Governmental jurisdictions

The Washington, DC, region is the home of federal scientific agencies (such as NASA, NOAA, and EPA) as well as significant universities (University of Maryland, Georgetown, Johns Hopkins, American University). Leveraging the proximity of those institutions could provide substantial capability to assemble data about the region based on GIS mapping, satellite photography and infrared sensors. All this only provides a snapshot of the region at the present time, which can support development of baseline information against which transformation might be measured. But as a core of a curriculum and research program, the available resources could be used: (a) to equip students with the analytical skills necessary for careers in environmental and regional assessment; and (b) as the basis for an annual "state of the region" report designed to catalyze discussion about the region's future.

Second, Virginia Tech could use its convening power to initiate a broad-based discussion about the future of governance relative to the challenges of transformation.

Some of the institutional capacity and framework that might have been useful to develop long-range planning toward the goal of sustainability has been neglected, weakened, or dismantled in the past three decades. Some of it, such as coherent land use planning, has never taken root in the United States. But transformation in the directions suggested in this essay will require an enhanced capacity to do long-range regional planning and the powers necessary to implement those plans. This, in turn, will require an unusually robust civic dialogue across political boundaries and regulatory jurisdictions to develop the governmental wherewithal and market mechanisms necessary to transformation. How market mechanisms, much favored at present, intersect with public decisions and regulatory rulings is itself a portentous and interesting subject that might form the core of a curriculum joining public policy, law, and planning. A few essential questions include:

- What is the proper balance between the public interest and private rights?
- By what combination of pricing, taxation, moral suasion, and regulation do we arrest environmental degradation and the loss of natural capital?
- How do we balance the legitimate interests of future generations with genuine needs of the present generation?
- By what analytical tools (public health data, pricing, discounting, least-cost, end-use analysis etc.) do we evaluate progress toward transformation?

The emerging educational institution, with energetic leadership, might catalyze a dialogue that engages the public, government officials, media, nonprofit organizations, and other academic institutions in the region with results that resound throughout the country.

Third, the physical facilities of the campus ought to be developed as a model of ecological design, including standards such as:

- Application of LEED standards to achieve high-performance buildings
- Maximum energy efficiency
- Maximal use of solar energy
- Climate neutrality
- Zero-discharge (purify wastewater on site)
- Use of third-party certified environmentally preferable materials and goods
- Elimination of toxic materials
- Management and monitoring of efficient energy and materials use
- Local purchase of food and materials to help jump-start a sustainable regional economy
- Encouraging use of public transport
- Providing incentives to minimize use of cars
- Composting organic wastes
- Natural landscaping

Most important, the development of the campus as a laboratory for ecological design in fields of architecture, engineering, landscape architecture, materials science, ecological engineering, and renewable energy technologies makes problems of sustainability manageable at a comprehensible scale and readily transferable into curriculum and research projects.

The building program for the Lewis Center at Oberlin College, for example, was developed through a series of public design charettes with some 250 students, faculty, and townspeople involved. The building operations, monitoring, and evolution, similarly, are parts of a curriculum in ecological design that includes fields of ecological engineering, landscape management, restoration ecology, renewable energy, building analysis, and data display. Beyond the Lewis Center itself, the results include establishment of a new start-up company to provide building analysis and display systems, a $10.6 million commercial construction project, and the Cleveland Green Building coalition. The launch of a new institution is an opportunity to build ecological design and design education in from the outset rather than add it later as an afterthought.

Typically, those who argue against building to high performance standards do so on the basis of purported costs. But data from a growing body of case studies shows, to the contrary, that high performance design comes in at or even below the costs of conventional construction while lowering life-cycle costs and improving performance. In other words, universities can't afford not to build green. Highly energy-efficient buildings deploying passive designs and photovoltaic systems also provide insurance against volatile energy costs.

Fourth, for transformation toward the goal of sustainability, the institution's buying and investment should support the transition toward a sustainable local economy, buying from local farms, businesses, and manufacturers, with a strong preference for those that are operated sustainably. There are many reasons for doing so.

Food in the United States, for example, is said to be transported approximately 1,500 miles from where it is grown to where it is eaten at a net investment of 11 calories of fossil energy for every calorie on the plate. Agricultural practices underlying the food system, further, are implicated in creation of a dead zone the size of the state of New Jersey in the Gulf of Mexico, degradation of the Chesapeake Bay, the drawdown of the Ogallala aquifer, the overuse of antibiotics, a long list of ecological and human problems associated with confinement feeding operations, issues of decency arising from abuse of farm laborers, ongoing soil loss, and an epidemic of obesity.

This system is not sustainable, which is to say that it will not be robust in a world of rising oil costs and increasing climate instability. Many of the same effects of the energy/climate transition will affect other businesses, providing good reason to use the buying and investment power of the northern Virginia campus to support the development of networks of sustainably operated suppliers. The supply system could provide material for a remarkable series of courses, case studies, and research across disciplinary boundaries.

Fifth, implementation of a transformative role for the northern campus is an opportunity to rethink a good bit of the conventional wisdom about education in order to recalibrate institutional imperatives, dynamics, operational procedures, and faculty incentives with the goal of catalyzing sustainability in the metropolitan region. Those intending to build an institution dedicated to transformation will have to rethink a great many of the old assumptions about careers in higher education, how the institution organizes itself as a "learning community," and how it can encourage vision across disciplinary boundaries. However defined, the goal of regional transformation will require an incentive structure (hiring, tenure, promotion, salaries) that encourages faculty innovation, boldness, and intellectual agility. It also will require more fluid communication throughout the entire institution.

The goal of catalyzing transformation, finally, will require a different kind of governance from that typical of colleges and universities. Trustees typically are elected or appointed because of prominence in business, law, or public affairs. Rarely, however, are they conversant with the larger issues of the time that underly the very need for transformation. Presidents, provosts, and deans, similarly, are not always selected for their vision, boldness, and commitment to transformation, but rather for their skill in maintaining institutional stability and their success in raising large amounts of money. Many are badly confused or poorly informed about the merely scientific evidence underlying the case for transformation. The goal of catalyzing transformation is sufficiently beyond the experience of most selected for leadership at either level, that it would be worthwhile to make special efforts to raise awareness and the level of shared information underlying the vision of transformation.

Conclusion

Wilson (2003) calls the years ahead a "bottleneck," a difficult and problematic transition. Rees (2003), Britain's Astronomer Royal believes that our odds of making this intact are less than 50-50. We have entered the rapids of humankind's long evolutionary career, and what lies ahead is anyone's guess. The combination of biotic impoverishment, climate change, growing poverty, and the means of mass disruption and destruction make this time in history like no other. The question before us is how educational institutions might quickly become a positive force to help negotiate the trials and opportunities of this transition without jettisoning the achievements and hard-won victories of the past and move on to a future better than that otherwise in prospect.

References

Benyus, Janine M. 2002. Biomimickry: Innovation Inspired by Nature. New York: Harper Perennial.

Campbell, Collin. 2004. The Coming Oil Crisis. London: Multi-Science Publishing Co. Ltd.

Deffeyes, Kenneth S. 2003. Hubert's Peak: The Impending World Oil Shortage. Princeton, NJ: Princeton University Press.

Millennium Ecosystem Assessment. 2005. Ecosystems and Human Well-Being: A Synthesis. Washington: Island Press

Powlson, David. 2005. Climatology: Will soil amplify climate change? Nature. 433 (7023): 204.

Rees, Martin. 2004. Our Final Hour: A Scientist's Warning: How Terror, Error and Environmental Disaster Threaten Humankind's Future in This Century -- On Earth and Beyond. New York: Basic Books.

Rees, William and Mathis Wackernagel. 1995. Our Ecological Footprint: Reducing Human Impacts on the Earth. Gabriola Island, BC: New Society Publishers

Watson, R.T. and the Core Writing Team. 2001. IPCC Third Assessment Report: Climate Change 2001. Geneva: International Panel on Climate Change.

Wilson, Edward O. 2003. The Future of Life. New York: Vantage Press.

Chapter 3
The University and Sustainable Regional Industries

David J. Hess

Increasingly, metropolitan regions that have experienced the negative side effects of sprawl, congestion, superstores, and automobile-dependent transportation are turning toward transit-oriented development, mixed-used buildings, urban growth boundaries, compact development, and other strategies associated with new urbanism and smart growth planning. Although changes in land use and infrastructure policies are important, they would do little good if the major industries of a region remained unconnected to regional greening initiatives. A comprehensive approach to regional sustainability needs to examine how regional industries can be brought into the process of building a sustainable metropolitan region. Because industries increasingly are linked to universities for research and development, the problem of developing new industries or changing old ones at a regional level is closely tied to the innovation potential of the region's universities.

Throughout the 20th century, universities have played a crucial role in developing new knowledges and technologies for both industry and the military (Kevles 1997; Leslie 1993; Noble 1977). However, the increase of global competition during the last decades of the 20th century pressed manufacturing industries in high-income countries to focus on constant innovation and high technology, and as a result, universities increasingly have emphasized research and teaching goals related to industrial innovation (Kleinman 2003). The passage of the Bayh-Dole Act of 1980, which allowed universities to capture revenue from patents and licenses, was an important historical marker of the increasing role that universities have played in economic development (Slaughter and Leslie 1997).

Both national and subnational regional policies have become oriented toward the model of the "technopole" or "triple helix" – that is, the synergistic development of state, university, and industrial partnerships through dense networks and regional clusters (Castells and Hall 1994; Leydesdorff and Etzkowitz 1997; see also Schach's chapter in this volume). The clusters link the strategic goals of universities with regional industrial strengths, and they provide a new source of state and industrial funding for university-based research. In turn, the advantages of dense informal networks, which the university-government partnerships can nurture, make it attractive for industries to locate in a particular region. The result is the paradoxical combination of globalization processes and a renewed emphasis on regional clusters.

Many regions across the world now seek to model their regional economies on Silicon Valley and similar high-technology clusters, such as Boston's Route 128 and the United

Kingdom's Cambridgeshire. To emulate those clusters and to create new variants of the triple helix, universities have developed strategic goals around emergent areas of high-technology research and development such as information technology, biotechnology, and nanotechnology.

To a large extent, the emergent areas of research and industrial innovation have developed without significant concern for environmental issues. There is some interest in configuring the new technological innovation clusters in ways that may address environmental problems, such as the use of biotechnology in environmental remediation or of nanotechnology in fuel cells. However, frequently the new technologies have also been the target of environmental concerns, such as campaigns against the toxic metals in computers, protests against genetically modified food, and growing concerns about the environmental and health implications of some nanotechnological materials. Yet, there is also the potential for developing environmental technology as a focus of research, development, and regional industry. This chapter probes the concept of what a sustainable regional industry can mean through a comparative discussion of various models.

Conceptual Background

Before discussing various opportunities and problems that face the university in defining a sustainable regional economy, the concepts of sustainability and globalization need to be clarified. Like apple pie, "sustainability" is a value that few people oppose in principle. It points in the direction of a desirable future and a legacy that present generations would, in principle, like to leave to their progeny. However, the term is highly subject to greenwashing, and it has come to mean almost anything. As a result, I have found in beneficial, in both teaching and research, to break the concept down along two dimensions.

The environmental dimension spans a spectrum of positions from incremental remediation of environmental hazards and existing pollution problems to the upstream world of design innovation that has a goal of nearly zero waste across a product's life cycle. In other words, although most of the time "sustainability" is translated into incremental projects of amelioration or remediation, in some cases people and firms have accepted the more profound challenge of developing product life cycles that begin almost entirely as waste products, consume few resources while being used, and can be converted to inputs into new products at the end of the life cycle (Pauli 1998; Todd and Todd 1993).

A second dimension of sustainability involves the argument that a truly sustainable society is not possible without addressing issues of social justice. In turn, the "justice" dimension also spans a spectrum of positions advocating everything from incremental poverty alleviation and the remediation of rights violations to more profound changes in economic and political institutions to make them more inclusive and democratic (see Fischer's chapter in this volume). Large corporations tend to work with a narrow definition of sustainability that focuses on the remediation of existing environmental problems, such as emissions from fossil fuels, whereas social movement organizations tend to articulate a vision of "just sustainability" that combines environmental and justice issues (see Agyeman, Bullard, and Evans 2003; McGranahan and Satterthwaite 2000).

As with the concept of sustainability, the concept of globalization needs clarification. Globalization as an empirical process that can be elucidated by research is frequently confused with globalism, a neoliberal political ideology that celebrates a corporate-led form of globalization as a political goal. In some cases, the social science literature falls prey to some of the assumptions of globalism, and the literature can become celebratory. In contrast, globalization will be understood here to mean historical changes that are continuous with the emergence of modernity in the 15th through 18th centuries but took distinct forms in the second half of the 20th century.

Within the political system, the nation-state has become embedded in an increasingly dense political field of international governmental and nongovernmental organizations, regional trading blocs and superstates, and subnational regional political entities, including "global cities" (Sassen 2000). Within the economic system, the economy has become much more internationalized, but claims about internationalization of the economy can be overstated in comparison with earlier historical periods (Hirst and Thompson 1999). Among the more significant changes that occurred during the late 20th century are the internationalization and digitalization of financial markets and manufacturing, the rise of post-Fordist production, and an increase in within-nation inequality in many countries, including the United States (Harvey 1989; Schmitt 2000). In the social and cultural systems, proportions of immigration to some countries may not have increased (Hirst and Thompson 1999), but the ethnic mix often has become more diversified in comparison with immigration patterns in the 19th and early 20th centuries. The diversification of national populations and the maintenance of diasporic ties through new information and communication technologies are among the factors that have contributed to a fragmentation of identity and a decline in the power of national identity as a mobilizing force in politics (Inda and Rosaldo 2001). Although there are many exceptions to the trends, they will be taken here as the points of departure for an empirically grounded concept of globalization (Hess 2007).

In the United States, as in many other countries, manufacturing and other industrial sectors face strong competition from low-income countries, including countries that also have better endowments of natural resources for some industries. As a result, the value of achieving "sustainability" often is framed in conflict with the value of economic viability and employment. The environment-versus-jobs framing of the issue tends to mobilize labor to the side of industry and therefore weaken the potential for blue-green coalitions (Gould, Lewis, and Roberts 2004). As a result, environmental values and politics tend to be championed by social movements, nongovernmental organizations, and community groups. Although everyone recognizes that sustainability, like universal health care coverage, would be "nice" to have, divisions occur over the extent to which it is "too expensive," especially in an era of global competition and pressures on the revenue base for governments.

Social movements play an important role in the politics of sustainability by putting pressure on the state and large, publicly traded corporations to remediate their environmental practices. In addition, social movements play a role in pioneering new technologies, such as organic food production and renewable energy (Hess 2005). Movements can draw attention to the politics of design and create conflicts over the definitions of objects that the private sector is putting into circulation, such as over genetically modified food and nuclear energy (Hess 2004). Furthermore, movements can help create markets for alternative products and for alternative forms of organizational control, such as locally grown food from locally owned farms. They also help remind analysts that the greening of regional industries is not merely driven by the triple helix of university-industry-government partnerships, but it also can have a grassroots dimension that taps into the power of civil society organizations and articulates a "just sustainability" vision of sustainability.

By viewing the greening of regional industries as a complex political process that cannot be completely captured by the logic of industrial innovation policy, it is possible to see some opportunities that might not otherwise be evident. Among the opportunities are the potential for greening the regional economy not only through major industries but also through small businesses and the productive activity of the nonprofit sector. As will become evident, a localist model of regional sustainability emerges alongside a technopole model.

Greening Existing Industrial Clusters

Most regional economies have an industrial focus, such as automobiles, software, entertainment, finance, chemicals, food processing, defense, and tourism. One of the first challenges of a program to green the regional economy is to motivate existing industries to undergo a greening process. In some cases, such as the chemical industry of Louisiana, the greening of a regional industrial cluster is a contentious political issue (Allen 2003). Yet, even where there is not a widely recognized problem associated with existing industries, the firms are likely to resist proposals for the ecological modernization of their production practices, technologies, and products. For-profit firms tend to resist environmental changes in production because the changes are seen as expensive and unprofitable. Likewise, high levels of environmental regulatory scrutiny in high-income countries have been cited as a key factor behind the decision of some industries to relocate manufacturing to low-income countries with lax regulations. Because firms historically have viewed the relationship between environmentally oriented changes in production and profitability as a zero-sum trade-off, they have often resisted changes and only made them when social movement campaigns or state regulations have forced them to do so.

Comparative analyses have shown that regulatory push remains the crucial factor in motivating industries to undertake environmentally oriented changes in their production practices (Bayliss, Connell, and Flynn 1998a, 1998b). Although regulatory push (and behind it, social movement activity) has been and probably remains the main factor behind whatever trends toward ecological modernization of industry can be found in most countries, there is considerable variation across industries and countries. For example, in many countries the chemical industry has undergone significant regulatory scrutiny, and it has been subjected to greater pressure to change industrial practices than most other industries. Likewise, pressures to undergo environmentally oriented reforms in production technologies and products have been much stronger in Western Europe than in the United States. In cases such as the Dutch chemical industry, partnerships among civil society organizations, the state, and corporations have led to significant reforms (Mol 1995). Such reforms are to some extent reversible; that is, they are subject to retrenchment as political climates change, and consequently the role of civil society pressure on both industry and government regulatory policies is crucial to maintaining and deepening the ecological modernization of industry.

In addition to regulatory push, a second strategy for motivating the greening of existing industries is through the profitability pull of "eco-efficient" innovations. A growing literature challenges the assumption of a trade-off between the greening of industrial production and lowered profitability (DeSimone and Popoff with the World Business Council for Sustainable Development 1997; Porter and van der Linde 1995). Likewise, a new industry of consultants, university researchers, and other specialists provides expertise for industries that are willing to view environmentally oriented changes as investments that bring direct financial returns as well as returns to brand and corporate image. For example, by "closing the loops" of manufacturing waste, firms may be able to reduce waste disposal costs and capture profits from waste reuse (Hawken, Lovins, and Lovins 1999).

In practice, however, eco-innovation can have very ambiguous environmental implications. For example, a furniture factory may invest in new cogeneration technology that allows it to divert wood shavings from a landfill by recycling them on-site for heating and electricity generation via incineration. The ultimate environmental effects (landfilling versus burning) may be ameliorative or destructive, depending on how clean the wood shavings are and the quality of emissions controls in the cogeneration plant, and how the emissions and greenhouse gases compare with the displaced, grid-based fuel sources. However, because the motivation is more cost savings than environmental amelioration, the broader environmental impacts are not crucial to the decision to "green" the technology. It is a cost-reduction decision that may have environmental benefits, but it may not.

Unfortunately, to date firms have not been convinced that a dramatic rethinking of product life cycles is in their best interest, and likewise governments have been unable to resist private-sector pressure to reverse or at a minimum enact weak environmental legislation. As a result, from the perspective of continued ecological degradation, neither regulatory push nor profitability pull have been sufficient to result in widespread ecological modernization of industry. Although there are some success stories, to date technological changes in industry have not been able to keep up with increased overall production and consumption, and with them the "treadmill" of growing deposits and withdrawals into the environment (Schnaiberg and Gould 1994).

The various models discussed in the remainder of this chapter need to be contextualized against the broader need to address unsustainable practices in a wide variety of existing industries, including existing regional industrial clusters. The net environmental impact of the various models discussed, in terms of aggregate measures such as global greenhouse gas emissions or release of toxic chemicals into the global ecosystem, would only be environmentally significant if they achieve widespread adoption. However, the models do provide opportunities for new university-community-industry partnerships, new employment possibilities, and the enhancement of the quality of life at a regional level. The localist variants also begin to address some of the fundamental issues underlying patterns of ownership associated with the continued treadmill of economic growth and environmental destruction that industrial societies have generated.

The Green Technopole

The idea of a "green" technopole can be viewed as an extension of the pattern of university-industry-government partnerships that are occurring in other sectors, such as information technology, biotechnology, and nanotechnology. It is difficult to identify a "green technopole" in the United States that could be compared with the information technology and biotechnology clusters in the San Francisco Bay area and Boston, but there are signs of energy innovation clusters developing in some areas.

One energy innovation cluster is developing in the San Francisco Bay Area, where Stanford University has established the Global Climate and Energy Project. Supported Exxon Mobil, General Electric, Toyota, and Schlumberger, the $225 million project will develop "clean energy" technologies and technologies to control greenhouse gases (Blumenstyk 2003).

San Jose State University and the Redevelopment Agency of the City of San Jose have also sponsored an Environmental Business Cluster, which has assisted more than 80 firms to develop new, environmentally oriented technologies, and there are other business incubators and support organizations for clean technology development in the region (Environmental Business Cluster 2005; WestStart-Calstart 2005). The rapid growth of the Bay Area cluster suggests the continued vitality of the entrepreneurial environment of Silicon Valley, which has been able to withstand various rapid transformations in the information technology industry (Saxenian 1996) and now is expanding into the environmental technology industry. In this context, private investment from venture capital firms is crucial for the early capitalization of new firms, which develop according to entrepreneurial models established in other industries.

A similar cluster also is under development in the New York capital district (Albany-Schenectady-Troy-Saratoga), where the state government has played a significant role. The New York State Energy Research and Development Authority, the New York State government, University at Albany, and Saratoga Economic Development Corporation are among the partners contributing to the development of the Saratoga Technology + Energy Park, which has a focus on clean energies (New York State Energy Research and Development Authority 2005). The state government also has partnered with Rensselaer Polytechnic Institute (2005) to open a $20 million Center for Future Energy Systems, that focuses on hydrogen fuel cells, energy conservation, and renewable energy technologies. Synergies also are developing with firms such as Plug Power, MTI MicroFuel cells, and General Electric's Global Research center, which is headquartered in the region.

Although evidence is still sketchy for the existence of a green technopole of similar scope to the more established technopoles in information technology, in general the model for advanced energy technology development appears to follow the key elements of other technologies. First, research funds draw on partnerships among state governments, universities, large corporations, and federal funding agencies. Second, technology development and diffusion occurs either through development by existing corporations, such as General Electric under its "eco imagination program," or from start-up companies that shift from venture capital to public stock offerings as they develop. Third, the manufactured products may be sold on local markets, especially during early testing and market development stages, but the intention is to develop industries that are "export-oriented" in the sense of marketing products beyond the region to national and global markets.

Opportunities for the development of regional industry clusters around innovative energy technologies can encounter object conflicts – that is, definitional struggles over the boundaries of what a desirable alternative or new technology should encompass. Such conflicts emerge particularly when environmental organizations challenge state governments and federal funders over priorities for new energy research. Categories such as renewable, clean, green, and future energy capture different formulations of desirable industrial futures, and with them priority areas for research funding and technology development. For example, a region may focus on renewable energy that generates only minimal pollution or environmental side effects (e.g., solar and wind) versus the development of hydrogen-powered automobiles. The latter may significantly clean up carbon emissions at the tailpipe, but hydrogen production is likely to be based on distributed reformulation from natural gas rather than renewable energy sources, and consequently the efficiency and net environmental impact is dubious. Nevertheless, in order to get the industrial buy-in that will be needed to move hydrogen beyond the demonstration project stage, it is likely that natural gas companies will need to be enlisted to provide backing from an influential part of the energy industry.

More broadly, "green" energy research and development can run the spectrum from wind-powered electric vehicles to plug-in electric hybrids with biofuels, natural-gas powered vehicles, hydrogen fuel cells, carbon sequestration technologies for "clean" coal, and the rebirth of nuclear energy as a "clean" energy. Within this field of contenders for the banner of "green" or "clean" energy, environmental movement organizations have divided over various issues, including the need to resurrect nuclear energy and the impact of wind farms on human viewsheds and avian fly-ways. Yet, it is clear that funding agencies and some firms are investing in research and development for the new technologies, and universities will play a key role in generating the research needed to overcome technical barriers.

The Green Technopole and Import Substitution

The concept of "import substitution" is well known in economics, and it also has been employed in the regional and urban studies literature for some time (e.g., Jacobs 1969; Shuman 2000). In this context, import substitution implies developing a regional economy by replacing goods that have been produced elsewhere with goods that have been produced locally. The locally produced goods may be sold locally, or they may be marketed more broadly. As applied to the advanced energy technologies of the green technopole, import substitution can be a valuable resource for capitalization and testing in the early stages of a product's development. By developing local markets for a new product, firms can stay close to users, work out problems, and have an incipient revenue stream. Primary examples of import substitution in the energy field involve substituting fossil fuels that are imported into a region for greener fuels that are produced locally.

Perhaps the most successful example of import substitution and green technopole development is the solar industry of Freiburg, Germany. Activism surrounding the Whyl nuclear power plant eventually led to a solar-oriented urban policy that directed the municipal utility to develop greater solar energy use. Triple-helix dynamics emerged in 1981 with the founding of the university-affiliated Fraunhofer Institute for Solar Energy Systems (2005), which works closely with the Albert Ludwig University. The city government spurred development by purchasing solar units in municipal buildings, and in 1992 it required future housing and municipal buildings to use passive and active solar energy (Solar Region Freiburg 2003). In 1995 the International Solar Energy Society (2005) moved its headquarters to the city, and in 1997 Solar-Fabrik, a solar module manufacturer, also moved to the city (Solar Region Freiburg 2005). A major shift in scale occurred in 1999, when the Federal Ministry of Economics and Technology inaugurated the 100,000 Roofs Solar Energy Power Program, which provided loans for solar panels. The program lasted until 2003 and resulted in about 345 MW of new solar capacity, an impressive quantity that established Germany as the leader of solar energy in Europe (International Energy Agency 2004; German Solar Industry Association 2004). Once again, the role of government – here both national and local – was crucial for the development of the industry.

In the United States, some states have renewable energy portfolio standards, and an increasing number of utilities have optional green pricing programs. By increasing the demand for renewable energy through mandates or voluntary price premia, utility companies can develop a revenue stream that helps pay for a shift of their energy mix to renewable sources. In cases where the utility is publicly owned, the new energy sources can be owned by the public utility. For example, Sacramento Municipal Utility District owns wind and solar farms that produce energy for its customers (Hess and Winner 2005). Even investor-owned utilities can be pushed to develop local renewable energy sources. For example, in the case of San Francisco, the investor-owned utility fought a grassroots effort to convert ownership to a public utility, and as a result of the defeat the city is now developing a "community choice" program (Hess and Winner 2005). The program aggregates consumers and seeks bids from energy providers that meet guidelines for both price and new renewable energy sources.

In many cases, new renewable energy sources are purchased through contracts with energy-generating facilities that are not locally owned. In other words, there is no necessary link between import substitution and the development of new firms in the region, let alone new manufacturing firms. Local firms can develop around installation of distributed energy, such as solar panels, and around ownership of wind farms. In San Francisco, the proposed community choice contracts will be combined with the city bond authority to mandate 360 MW of new capacity and load reductions, including new solar and wind generation. Assuming that new firms arise from the mandate, it is likely that solar installation companies and other service provision firms will be the primary new industry. However, as in the case of Freiburg, it is possible also that solar manufacturing firms may relocate to the region.

A similar pattern of import substitution can occur with regional transit companies. For example, Alameda County Transit of the East Bay of California has been developing hydrogen fuel-cell powered buses that, while still in the experimental stage, have helped to develop a California business in partnership with the state of California, Chevron-Texaco, and an international bus manufacturer (Hess and Winner 2005). Likewise, in Chattanooga a cluster emerged around the regional transit agency, an electric vehicle research institute (now the Advanced Transit Technology Institute), the Tennessee Valley Authority, research programs at the University of Tennessee, and an electric vehicle manufacturer that originated with contracts from the city to make electric buses instead of purchasing new diesel buses made elsewhere. The eastern Tennessee cluster has some significant innovations, including the all-electric downtown circulator in Chattanooga, which runs on electricity that is primarily generated from hydropower. In both cases, transit agencies leveraged their procurement power to help establish new regional businesses via import substitution. In the Chattanooga case, the electric bus company eventually failed, but our research indicates that the failure occurred after it attempted to expand too rapidly from its original manufacturing niche (Hess and Winner 2005).

Biofuels are another example of import substitution that can help spur the development of regional industries. Federal mandates (such as the ethanol standard), state government mandates (such as those in Minnesota), and procurement policies (such as city fleet targets) all contribute to new demand for biofuels. By shifting a portion of fuel to biodiesel, public transit agencies can help develop a regional refining industry, and city and state fleets can utilize ethanol mixes in their gasoline-powered vehicles. Because biofuels are considered to be carbon neutral and to have lower and less toxic emissions than standard petroleum-based fuels, overall impact on the environment may be reduced. Even if their net environmental impact is moot, biofuels currently are considered advantageous because they reduce dependence on foreign petroleum and can help develop regional industries.

The three examples of energy-based import substitution are consistent with the triple helix structure of environmental technology manufacturing, but there are two significant differences. First, there is a greater diversity of ownership patterns. New, export-oriented manufacturing firms can emerge as biofuels refiners and bus and solar panel manufacturers. Their products may be consumed locally during initial phases, but eventually are sold on national markets. In contrast, import substitution in the energy field can be linked to the development of locally owned energy production sites, such as locally owned distributed generation, a locally oriented installation industry, and publicly owned wind farms. Likewise, in some cases state governments have set up incentive programs that assist locally owned agricultural cooperatives to develop biorefining and wind farms (New Rules Project 2005).

A second difference is that the triple-helix dynamics of the technopole are less obvious in the more locally oriented forms of alternative energy production, except where manufacturing is involved, such as in the Chattanooga electric bus case. This is to be expected, because the state and universities are focused on developing high-tech industries that can produce new products for sale on global markets. As a result, the pattern of green energy development based on import substitution is continuous on one end with the green technopole and, on the other end, with a model of locally owned production for primarily local consumption, or what I term "green localism." The latter model also can play a role in a general strategy of regional economic development, and it is especially prominent in the waste and food industries.

Waste-Based Import Substitution

Another type of import substitution converts waste products into inputs for a new production process or into reusable consumables. The remanufacturing industry is one example of waste-based import substitution, but to date the industry has not been configured into regional clusters with university-government-private sector partnerships. The demonstration projects of industrial ecology are perhaps the closest to a regional cluster of waste-based import substitution. The most well-known model of industrial ecology is the Kalunborg site in Denmark, where the by-products of a fossil-fuel burning electrical plant, such as ash, are utilized as inputs for other manufacturers that are located nearby. Colocation does not require immediate proximity, as in the Kalundborg site, and it can be expanded to a regional level. Universities can assist regional cluster development by inventorying wastes and inputs at a regional level to identify possible synergies for remanufacturing.

Industrial ecology has created some excitement in North America, and there are some cases of cities that have developed eco-industrial parks (Chernow 2002). However, to date most of the North American eco-industrial projects are either agricultural (such as composting operations) or in incipient stages of development. One problem is that waste regulations in the United States have made it difficult for reutilization of some waste products. A more general problem is that changes in one firm's production technologies can alter its waste by-products, which then places another firm at jeopardy in obtaining supplies. In other words, the industrial ecology model rests uneasily with the emphasis on constant innovation, especially of production processes, that is required for survival in a global economy. Although the problems can be surmounted, they also point to some of the hurdles that an industrial ecology approach must overcome (Desrochers 2001).

Another example of a demonstration project around industrial ecology is biologically based wastewater treatment. The systems developed by John Todd and associates at Ocean Arks demonstrate how wastewater can be treated by passing it through a variety of biological systems that eventually convert the waste products into life support (Todd and Todd 1993). In the process, a network of new businesses is made possible, including fish and other aquatic food, bait, decorative plants, edible plants, animal fodder, fertilizer, and water. By producing new plant and animal products from waste, it is possible not only to reduce the negative externalities caused by sinking waste into the environment but also to create a cluster of new businesses that substitute locally produced products from those obtained in distant markets.

A third opportunity for waste-based import substitution involves energy waste. A variety of businesses exist in this area, from the greening of new building construction to weatherization of existing buildings. Urban programs can be combined with poverty reduction goals – examples include the Green Affordable Housing Coalition (2004) and the home energy weatherization programs offered by some public utilities. Some states have public utilities dedicated to providing assistance for reduction in energy consumption (e.g., Efficiency Vermont 2003). To date, the programs have helped create a small-business sector of local contractors, but they have not yet moved to the next step of regional clusters with links to university research programs.

A fourth opportunity for waste-based import substitution involves the reuse of consumer products. An example is the resale industry, which is one of the most rapidly growing segments of the retail sector. Resale includes a variety of institutions: the informal economy of yard, rummage, and church sales; the 15,000 resale shops (including clothing, furniture, sporting goods, and electronic products); the thrift segment (such as Salvation Army and Goodwill Industries); and reuse companies, which sell reusable home construction products. Flea markets also have been used to redevelop urban spaces, including abandoned big box stores (Christensen 2005), and they can be combined with farmers' markets, craft fairs, and small business districts to revitalize urban areas. By aggregating small-scale vendors and locating them in resale retail clusters, new possibilities for economic development emerge that require relatively little capital investment from a city government or nonprofit organization. Resale clusters provide opportunities for entrepreneurship in the retail sector, and they provide opportunities for a regional economy to diversify its job base away from export-oriented manufacturing.

In some cases, reuse companies have developed a cluster of related businesses. For example, some of the used building materials or "reuse" centers have spun off side businesses that make furniture from recycled wood. Some also have developed an alternative to building demolition, which accounts for about two thirds of all solid waste. Deconstruction involves the careful dismantling of buildings, usually by hand and sometimes with teams of paid staff and volunteers. By substituting deconstruction for demolition, reuse centers can save up to 90 percent of building materials. When the reuse centers are set up as nonprofit organizations, the materials can be donated to the center, and frequently the employees are offered job training and skills development opportunities. Once the materials have been processed for resale, the products often are offered at steep discounts compared with those in new home furnishing stores, thereby benefiting low- and moderate-income families. Finally, proceeds can be used to fund low-income housing, as is being done in some of the Habitat for Humanity reuse centers. The reuse center model is now spreading across the country, and it provides another way in which an economically viable organizational form can bring together environmental and social justice goals (Hess and Winner 2005).

The resale industry mixes goals of environmental amelioration and poverty reduction, but within this broader field there are differences in the way the object of a "used good" is constituted. Thrift stores and to some extent the yard-sale economy are concerned with offering low prices for low- and moderate-income families, whereas some of the building and construction reuse stores have a more environmental orientation. Some of the reuse organizations have explicit missions that include both environmental and poverty-reduction goals. The variations in definitions of resale raise questions about what constitutes sustainability in these sectors. In the end, resale may result in little more than a delay of consumer goods on their trip to the landfill, particularly for clothing, sporting goods, and electronics. Resale generally does not address the fundamental issue of how to manufacture products so they can be remanufactured easily or landfilled without toxicity, although as resale grows it may help raise awareness of these issues. For example, building deconstruction experts note that the more recent buildings, with prefabricated materials and heavy use of glues, are much more difficult to deconstruct than older buildings. The specialists' work provides insights into how the construction process upstream might be redesigned to make long-term recycling of building materials more viable.

There is little academic research on the resale sector, but the developments represent tremendous opportunities for universities that are engaged in thinking through the possibilities of sustainability at a metropolitan level. Citizens have become increasingly concerned with quality-of-life issues, and those concerns often come to a head over plans for new retail developments. Planning board meetings can become contentious events, where citizens on both sides line up either for or against the latest development plan. Yet, in the end the disputes do little to answer the siren song of low prices and one-stop shopping that the big box superstores can offer. A resale district or a large flea market can become a vital ingredient in a metropolitan sustainability project. Clusters of locally owned, small remanufacturing firms – such as the furniture manufacturing businesses that have spun off the reuse centers – provide another model of how the reuse economy can be developed.

In the waste-based examples of import substitution, capitalization can occur through "donated" waste products that have lost their value to the original user. Because donations have value as a tax write-off, nonprofit organizations have flourished in this sector. There also is a vibrant informal economy around yard sales as well as a small-business sector around resale that can be self-capitalized through inventory growth of goods purchased at a steep discount or traded for future purchases. These alternative organizational forms co-exist with the larger and publicly traded businesses found in the remanufacturing industry.

Food-Based Import Substitution

The emergence of sustainable local agricultural networks is arguably the most well-developed form of a regional industrial cluster that is based on small, locally owned, privately held businesses and nonprofit organizations. Although not all of the food produced in such clusters is grown organically, in many cases food production utilizes fewer synthetic inputs, and in any case the environmental costs of long-distance transportation are reduced.

At the national and international levels, organic food production has become increasingly industrialized, but the locally oriented food networks have not disappeared. Instead, sustainable local food networks have grown alongside the nonlocal organic food industry (Guthman 2004; Hess 2004). Because consumers are concerned with food quality – due to preferences for food freshness, provenance, and safety – local food can command a price premium, as well as a shopping effort premium, in comparison with local manufactured goods. As a result, local ownership is more able to resist displacement by large, external firms that flood local markets with lower-priced products.

At an institutional level, local agricultural networks include community gardens, school gardens, community-supported agriculture farms, farmers' markets, retail food cooperatives, and restaurants and cafeterias that buy local food. Those organizations have become increasingly networked with anti-hunger and food security organizations, such as food banks, pantries, shelters, and related organizations (Gottlieb and Fisher 1996). For example, community gardens and small farms donate excess food, farmers' markets offer food stamps and food education programs, and community-supported agriculture farms offer low-income scholarships and food donations. Some organizations are nonprofit, but even the private-sector organizations tend to be small businesses that are not oriented toward profit growth. As a result, conditions are established for a more robust understanding of sustainability along the lines of sustainability with justice outlined above and in Agyeman, Bullard, and Evans (2003).

In addition to the broader interorganizational networks among the various types of local agricultural and food institutions, some of the institutions themselves are sites of interorganizational networking. For example, community gardens frequently have helped to revitalize a neighborhood, and they have become sites for political organizing (Hess and Winner 2005; Lawson 2005; von Hassell 2002). Likewise, farmers' markets and food cooperatives are not only sites of networking among farmers and local consumers, but they also can draw people into a neighborhood and be colocated with small businesses.

City and regional governments can help develop local agricultural networks through a variety of strategies. For example, community gardens increasingly face land tenure issues as neighborhoods undergo revitalization and land values increase. Some cities are also finding that community gardening can be incorporated into the mission of parks and school grounds, where gardening can diversify park and recreational usage, increase the safety of publicly used areas, and contribute to the educational mission of public schools (Hess and Winner 2005). Likewise, in some cases city governments have encouraged the development of the networks by providing space and other resources for farmers' markets. In California, local governments can certify farmers as bona-fide local or state-level producers, and likewise they can certify farmers' markets to prevent resale from farmers and influx from out-of-state farmers. Federal legislation in the 1970s also allowed Cooperative Extension Services to help build farmers' markets, and their efforts helped spur the growth of the institution from about 300 markets nationally in 1970 to about 3,000 markets 30 years later (Brown 2001, 2002).

The emergence of direct-to-consumer marketing probably will not be adequate to maintain small farms located close to suburban areas and subject to increasing land values. It is likely that the only solution for farms in such a situation is conversion to nonprofit organizations that grow food to support other goals such as providing food to the hungry, preserving green spaces, and developing educational programs for schools. The emergence of nonprofit farming should be viewed not as the last gasp of the family farm but as the emergence of a new type of institution that could be an important player in a sustainable regional economy and an overall plan for green-space utilization. Not only are new technologies – organic and intensive food cultivation – necessary for the preservation of farms in areas proximate to large cities, but so are new organizational forms.

As in the other fields, in agriculture there will be ongoing definitional conflicts over what the "greening" of agriculture will mean. Again, object conflicts emerge among types of "green agriculture" and the choices involved in how one is to define and design a process for greening agriculture at an urban level. At one extreme, sustainable agriculture involves seed saving, composting, and organic and manual inputs, whereas at the other extreme there are incremental changes in the food production system that creates processed foods that are less unhealthy or more "natural." The later may include some organic ingredients, but more often it involves some claim related to food processing techniques, such as the absence of transfatty acids or partially hydrogenated oils.

Consumers face trade-offs among a range of products, from locally grown, fresh, whole foods to processed, frozen, nonlocal organic to processed "natural" foods. The point of consumption becomes a site where opportunities exist to embed local, whole, and organic foods in the regional economy, but ultimately those battles need to be carried from the farmers' market to the supermarket. For local, organic agricultural networks to survive and prosper, the purchasing policies of supermarkets will need to be redirected toward local, organic sources. This challenge is as true for the conventional supermarkets as it is for the new, upscale natural food supermarket chains. As a product, food no longer is merely a technology driven entity that meets a code standard of organic or nonorganic; the challenge for a sustainable regional economy also is to define its provenance.

Opportunities exist for universities to define public missions around sustainability and agriculture. With some exceptions, at the major land grant universities organic agricultural research has remained a low priority, and social science research on local food networks can hardly be considered a high-prestige subfield in the social sciences. Unlike the energy field, where there are significant corporate and government investments being made in clean and renewable energy, the public domain quality of organic agriculture inputs has made the field relatively unattractive to corporate investors. As a result, there is little evidence for triple helix dynamics in this field, but there are significant educational opportunities for university programs oriented toward local networks of food, agriculture, and food security.

Other Sectors

Although it is not possible to comprehensively cover the potential for building a sustainable regional economy across all industries, it is worth mentioning some of the possibilities in a few other, related sectors. In the three remaining sectors that will be mentioned here, it is more difficult to identify specific "greening" processes, but there are processes related to import substitution that provide some of the groundwork for a vision of a sustainable regional economy that includes a justice dimension.

Health issues intersect with sustainability in a variety of ways at a regional level. Health considerations, especially when industrial exposure is distributed unevenly across ethnic and class divides, can provide a powerful framework to tip public opinion and political will in favor of changes that reduce exposure to toxic emissions from local brown industries. By aligning environmentally oriented import-substitution strategies with public health and environmental justice perspectives, it becomes much easier to mobilize the political will needed to develop import-substituting businesses and nonprofit organizations. In the health field, much of primary care delivery remains in the hands of locally owned, small provider practices, and consequently the opportunities for import substitution are less evident. However, the field of prevention, especially through dietary change associated with fresh (and local) food, might be conceptualized as a form of import substitution. In other words, through preventive health practices, dependency on drug-based imports to a regional economy can be reduced.

Media issues also intersect with local sustainability, largely through the politics of community diversity. The increasing control of electronic media in the hands of distant corporations has fueled a growing backlash in support of media reform as well as alternative media institutions such as community radio, Internet-based local media, public access television programming, and local alternative print media. Frequently, community media organizations are very concerned with building programming and coverage that represents the diversity of the community. Because environmental issues often have a significantly higher impact on low-income residents and ethnic minority communities, media that give them a voice will tend to provide a forum for environmental, justice, and environmental justice discussions within the community.

Finally, locally oriented financial reform can have an impact on building a sustainable regional economy. Although the dominant institutions of the regional political economy will be focused on the publicly traded corporations associated with export-oriented manufacturing clusters, there are many other opportunities available for import substitution in the realm of finance. Institutions such as credit unions, local currencies, buy-local business organizations, and microfinance institutions provide another opportunity for financing the innovations of an import-substituting green regional economy. Many small businesses that are not publicly held can benefit from the marketing, expertise, and financial support that are provided by alternative financial institutions and often not available from the increasingly consolidated commercial banking industry.

Conclusions

The logic of continued economic growth that underlies these ecological crises is driven by large, publicly traded corporations that must show continued short-term profitability in order to attract the continued interest and confidence of investors. The green technopole model of ecological modernization takes place largely inside the existing system. After initial start-up research and development funding from federal and state governments, sometimes in partnership with large corporations, it is expected that the next phase of development will be manufacturing firms that will require access to capital markets for growth and long-term viability. They may sell some products locally and therefore utilize an import substitution strategy, particularly during the early phases of product development, but the long-term trajectory is toward export-oriented sale of manufactured goods. Although the publicly traded firm is not the only possible form for the green technopole firm, the industries will tend to be oriented toward patentable research, manufacturing for nonlocal markets, corporate forms of organization, and capitalization from public stock offerings or the cash coffers of large corporations.

There are many advantages to developing environmental technology as a regional industry cluster. The industries will develop new technologies and products and provide high-income jobs as well as a source of revenue for the region. Because the problems of global warming and related energy issues are not likely to be solved in the short term, the industries are likely to offer a relatively stable economic base for the region. Furthermore, because the industries are in the business of making greener products, they are more likely to respond to threats to brand dilution caused by criticisms of pollution hazards from their production processes. As a result, they have the potential to generate not only greener products but greener production processes.

In other words, there is much to be said in favor of having a "green technopole" as the regional industrial base, especially in comparison with a brown or silicon technopole. However, because the industries of the green technopole will be oriented toward profit maximization, and because there is little or no regulatory push to ensure that the technological innovations and new products will be sustainable in a profound sense, the green technopole industries are likely to become caught in the contradiction of design choices that optimize profits and those that optimize environmental impact. As a result, the vision of environmental sustainability may become incremental and oriented toward remediation of existing environmental problems rather than a deeper rethinking of the entire product life cycle from a zero-waste perspective. Furthermore, because firms will focus on high-tech, high-skilled labor, providing employment opportunities to low-income neighborhoods likely will be a relatively low priority.

The strategy of import substitution in combination with local, small business ownership provides an alternative mechanism for capitalizing an alternative type of green industry clusters. Under green localism, the primary organizational form is the privately owned small business, nonprofit corporation, voluntary organization, or local government agency. Locally owned import substitution entails using local inputs in locally owned firms that produce primarily for the local economy (Shuman 2000; Williamson, Imbroscio, and Alperovitz 2002). Under a localist economic organization, there is less emphasis on growth and production for profit and greater emphasis on staying in business to provide a living. The sector tends to be undercapitalized, but it tends to provide a wider range of employment opportunities and product access to a broader segment of the population.

Furthermore, in the green localist form of the greening of regional industry, the vision of sustainability tends to be much broader than the model of incremental amelioration found in the corporate sector. The design of production practices can be altered dramatically – as in organic agriculture, distributed solar, and building deconstruction – to generate new products. Likewise, environmental concerns are often linked to community justice issues, such as through food security, energy assistance programs, and access to affordable home supplies and consumer goods. Because organizations are not dependent on short-term earnings reports for their continued existence, they are in a better position to resist the need for continued growth that is at the heart of the problem of the "treadmill" of ongoing economic growth and environmental degradation. With some help from local governments and universities, there is tremendous potential to develop clusters of firms and nonprofit organizations around the import-substituting, green, locally owned industries.

Although I have tended to emphasize the difference between the models of the green technopole and green localism, it should be clear that there are many interstitial forms and hybrids. For example, the Freiburg solar industry is an example of a green technopole that, at least initially, was producing for local markets via an import-substitution strategy. Likewise, through organizations such as the Business Alliance for Local Living Economies (2005), it is possible for small, locally owned businesses that have a sustainability and social justice mission to network with like-minded businesses to purchase products nationally and internationally. Regional governments do not need to choose between the green technopole or green localism; rather, they need to recognize the value of developing both simultaneously.

Likewise, the university has a role to play in each of the fields. The dominant attraction – what Bourdieu (1998) might call the "right hand" of the university – will be to the high-stakes finances associated with the green technopole and the development of partnerships with large corporations and the state to form new industries. The partnerships are very attractive to a university because they bring in revenue for applied research that has technology transfer potential. As a result, the university will tend to define sustainability and regional industrial development around some version of environmental technology, which to date has largely meant clean fuel and fuel cell research.

However, the role of the university in a sustainable regional economy can be much more broadly defined, and opportunities exist for the university to serve as the node in local networks around energy aggregation, public transit, resale, food, community health, community media, and community financial institutions. In an institution as diverse as the modern university, there is room for the left and right hands. Even if the portfolio of research projects on sustainability will be weighted toward the technopole projects, the university will serve itself and its community well by supporting a diverse range of research activities oriented toward sustainability and the metropolitan region.

For example, universities can play a role in facilitating network building among the various types of industries described here, they can provide inventories of waste products and needs, and they can build demonstration projects on the campus. Universities can also stretch easily downward in the educational system to the K-12 programs, where there are tremendous opportunities for building demonstration projects that also can serve as the basis for community-based research and recruitment of students into the university's undergraduate and graduate programs. By thinking about the issue of sustainability and regional development in a broad way to include a diverse range of regional industries, it is possible for the university not only to help develop the high-tech, green technopoles of the future but also to help develop a vision of just sustainability that articulates goals of zero waste production and the democratization of political decision making.

References

Agyeman, Julian, Robert Bullard, and Bob Evans. 2003. *Just Sustainabilities.* Cambridge, MA: MIT Press.

Allen, Barbara. 2003. *Uneasy Alchemy: Citizens and Experts in Louisiana's Chemical Corridor Disputes.* Cambridge, MA: MIT Press.

Bayliss, R., L. Connell, and A. Flynn. 1998a. Sector Variation and Ecological Modernization. Towards an Analysis at the Level of the Firm. *Business Strategy and the Environment* 7(3):150-161.

Bayliss, R., L. Connell, and A. Flynn.. 1998b. Company Size, Environmental Regulation, and Ecological Modernization: Further Analysis at the Level of the Firm. *Business Strategy and the Environment* 7(5):285–296.

Blumenstyk, Goldie. 2003. Greening the World or "Greenwashing" a Reputation? *Chronicle of Higher Education*, January 10, pp. A22–24.

Bourdieu, Pierre. 1998. *Acts of Resistance.* New York: The New Press.

Brown, Allison. 2001. Counting Farmers' Markets. *Geographical Review* 91(4):655–674.

Brown, Allison. 2002. Farmers' Market Research 1940-2000: An Inventory and Review. *American Journal of Alternative Agriculture* 17(4):167–176.

Business Alliance for Local Living Economies. 2005. About Us. Retrieved September 1, 2005 (www.livingeconomies.org/aboutus).

Castells, Manuel, and Peter Hall. 1994. *Technopoles of the World.* New York: Routledge.

Chernow, Martin. 2002. Introduction. *Bulletin Series: Yale School of Forestry and Environmental Studies* 106:9–22.

Christensen, Julia. 2005. How Communities are Re-Using the Big Box. Retrieved September 1, 2005 (www.bigboxreuse.com).

DeSimone, Livio, and Frank Popoff, with the World Business Council for Sustainable Development. 1997. *Eco-Efficiency: The Business Link to Sustainable Development*. Cambridge, MA: MIT Press.

Desrochers, Pierre. 2001. Eco-Industrial Parks: The Case for Private Planning. *Independent Review* 5(3):345–372.

Efficiency Vermont. 2003. 2003 Annual Report. Retrieved September 1, 2005 (www.efficiencyvermont.org/Docs/2003ExecutiveSummary.pdf).

Environmental Business Cluster. 2005. Environmental Business Cluster. Retrieved September 1, 2005 (www.environmentalcluster.org/Description.htm).

Fraunhofer Institute for Solar Energy Systems. 2005. History. Retrieved September 1, 2005 (www.ise.fhg.de/english/profile/history/index.html).

German Solar Industry Association. 2004. German Solar Market and Technology. Retrieved September 1, 2005 (www.bsi-solar.de/english/solar_market/index.asp).

Gottlieb, Robert, and Andrew Fisher. 1996. Community Food Security and Environmental Justice: Searching for a Common Discourse. *Agriculture and Human Values* 3(3):23–32.

Gould, Kenneth, Tammy Lewis, and J. Timmons Roberts. 2004. Blue-green Coalitions: Constraints and Possibilities in the Post 9-11 Political Environment. *Journal of World Systems Research* 10(1):91–116.

Green Affordable Housing Coalition. 2004. Our Mission. Retrieved October 20, 2004 (www.affordablegreenbuilding.org/).

Guthman, Julie. 2004. *Agrarian Dreams: The Paradox of Organic Farming in California*. Berkeley, CA: University of California Press.

Harvey, David. 1989. *The Condition of Postmodernity*. Oxford, UK: Blackwell.

Hawken, Paul, Amory Lovins, and J. Hunter Lovins. 1999. *Natural Capitalism*. Boston: Little, Brown, and Co.

Hess, David. 2004. Organic Food and Agriculture in the U.S.: Object Conflicts in a Health-Environmental Movement. *Science as Culture* 13(4):493–513.

Hess, David. 2005. Technology- and Product-Oriented Movements: Approximating Social Movement Studies and STS. *Science, Technology, and Human Values* 30(4): 515-535.

Hess, David. 2007. *Alternative Pathways in Science and Industry: Activism, Innovation, and the Environment in an Era of Globalization*. Cambridge, MA: MIT Press.

Hess, David, and Langdon Winner. 2005. Case Studies of Sustainability, the Politics of Design, and Localism. Retrieved September 1, 2005 (www.davidjhess.org/sustlocCasesTOC.html).

Hirst, Paul, and Graham Thompson. 1999. *Globalization in Question*. Second edition. Malden, MA: Blackwell/Oxford.

Inda, Jonathan, and Renato Rosaldo, eds. 2001. *The Anthropology of Globalization: A Reader*. Malden, MA: Blackwell/Oxford.

International Energy Agency. 2004. Germany: Photovoltaic Technology Status and Prospects. Photovoltaic Power Systems Programme. Country Summaries. Germany. Retrieved September 1, 2005 (www.oja-services.nl/iea-pvps/countries/germany/index.htm).

International Solar Energy Society. 2005. An Introduction to ISES. Retrieved September 1, 2005 (www.ises.org/isesintro.html).

Jacobs, Jane. 1969. *The Economy of Cities*. New York: Vintage.

Kevles, Daniel. 1997. *The Physicists*. New York: Vintage.

Kleinman, Daniel. 2003. *Impure Cultures: University Biology at the Millennium*. Madison, WI: University of Wisconsin Press.

Lawson, Laura. 2005. *City Bountiful: A Century of Community Gardening in the United States*. Berkeley, CA: University of California Press.

Leslie, Stuart. 1993. *The Cold War and American Science*. New York: Columbia.

Leydesdorff, Loet, and Henry Etzkowitz. 1997. A Triple Helix of University-Industry-Government Relations. In *Universities and the Global Knowledge Economy*, Henry Etzkowitz and Loet Leydesdorff (eds.). London and Washington: Pinter.

McGranahan and Satterthwaite. 2000. Environmental Health or Ecological Sustainability? Reconciling the Brown and Green Agendas in Urban Development. In *Sustainable Cities in Developing Countries*, Cedric Pugh (ed.), 73–90. London and Sterling, VA: Earthscan.

Mol, Arthur. 1995. *The Refinement of Production*. Utrecht, The Netherlands: International Books.

New Rules Project. 2005. Ethanol and Biodiesel Incentives: Missouri. Institute for Local Self Reliance. Retrieved September 1, 2005 (www.newrules.org/agri/mobiofuels. html).
New York State Energy and Development Authority. 2005. Saratoga Technology + Energy Park. Retrieved September 1, 2005 (www.nyserda.org/Programs/Economic_ Development/step.asp).

Noble, David. 1977. *America by Design*. Oxford, UK: Oxford University Press.

Pauli, Gunter. 1998. *The Road to Zero Emissions*. Sheffield, UK: Greenleaf Publishing.

Porter, Michael, and Claas van der Linde. 1995. Green and Competitive. *Harvard Business Review* 68(3):79–91.

Rensselaer Polytechnic Institute. 2005. Rensselaer Opens New $20 Million Center for Future Energy Systems. Retrieved September 1, 2005 (www.rpi.edu/web/Campus. News/features/061305-fescat.html).

Sassen, Saskia. 2000. *Cities in a World Economy*. Thousand Oaks, CA: Pine Forge/ Sage.

Saxenian, Annalee. 1996. *Regional Advantage: Culture and Competition in Silicon Valley and Route 128*. Cambridge, MA: Harvard University Press.

Schmitt, John. 2000. Inequality and Globalization: Some Evidence from the United States. In *The Ends of Globalization*, Don Kalb, Marco van der Lind, Richard Staring, Bart van Steenbergen, and Nico Wilterdink (eds.), 157–168. Lanham, MD: Rowman and Littlefield.

Schnaiberg, Allan, and Kenneth Gould. 1994. *Environment and Society*. New York: St. Martin's.

Shuman, Michael. 2000. *Going Local*. New York: Routledge.

Slaughter, Sheila, and Larry Leslie. 1997. *Academic Capitalism*. Baltimore: The Johns Hopkins University Press.

Solar Region Freiburg. 2003. Freiburg Solar City. Retrieved September 1, 2005 (www. solarregion.freiburg.de/solarregion/freiburg_solar_city.php).

Todd, Nancy, and John Todd. 1993. *From Eco-Cities to Living Machine*. Berkeley, CA:

North Atlantic Books.

Von Hassell, Malve. 2002. *The Struggle for Eden*. Westport, CT: Bergin and Garvey.

WestStart-Calstart. 2005. About Us. Retrieved September 1, 2005 (www.calstart.org/aboutus/whatisweststart.php?p=aboutus).
Williamson, Thad, David Imbroscio, and Gar Alperovitz. 2002. *Making a Place for Community*. New York: Routledge.

Chapter 4
Metropolitan Transformation through Restoration

Janice Cervelli Schach

For the first time in history, more than half of the earth's population lives in urban regions. In the United States, 80 percent of the population now lives in metropolitan regions, and the population is predicted to grow 23 percent by 2025. Urbanization at such a large scale and accelerated pace strains human and natural infrastructure considerably. The restoration of essential infrastructure through integrative development can serve to ensure the future of the metropolis.

Before anything new can be built anywhere in this new urban world, something else has to be fixed, preserved, or restored. This commercial engine is called the restoration economy: an economy based on revitalization of human-made and natural resources. Restoration development cuts across a wide range of interests, from health to hydrology, from materials engineering to historic preservation. The size of this worldwide economy is conservatively estimated at $2 trillion annually (Cunningham 2002.)

The Virginia Tech River Farm Sustainability Conversations pose the question, "What is the role of graduate education, research, and outreach in guiding the forthcoming transformation in ways that improve humankind?" This chapter explores how the growing restoration economy offers vast opportunities for universities to play a central role in the advancement of new approaches to environmental restoration.

One focus of the discussion is the Restoration Institute. The unique natural and architectural resources of the Lowcountry of South Carolina, combined with the academic expertise of Clemson University, present an ideal knowledge cluster dedicated to restoration research. The Clemson University Restoration Institute was established in 2004 to advance the establishment of such a cluster and knowledge in integrative approaches to the restoration of historic, ecological, and urban infrastructure.

The Restoration Institute and its role in the formation of such a restoration-related industry cluster within a large metropolitan area presents a possible model for how Virginia Tech's graduate programs in design, natural resources, planning, policy, and science/technology studies could possibly assume leadership in the transformation of the Washington, DC region.

The Restoration Challenge – Rebuilding Our Communities

Population growth and development sprawl are placing significant pressures on already overtaxed urban infrastructure throughout the United States. Much of the existing constructed infrastructure is decrepit, in need of replacement, and largely incapable of supporting such growth. The American Society of Civil Engineers' (ASCE) 2005 Infrastructure Report Card estimates a backlog of $1.6 trillion for rebuilding the national infrastructure including roads, bridges, transit systems, aviation, drinking water, sewer lines, and schools (ASCE 2005a). Many of these systems are inefficient, potentially detrimental to environmental and historical resources, and short-lived.

It is estimated that the drinking water and wastewater systems in the United States are facing replacement costs of nearly $1 trillion over the next 20 years (Water Infrastructure Network 2005) and an annual shortfall of $46 billion for infrastructure replacements just to meet existing federal water regulations. Redevelopment of urban and former industrial sites provides significant opportunities, but requires significant remediation. In 2004, the Environmental Protection Agency (EPA) estimated there are a total of 350,000 waste sites in the United States that will cost up to $250 billion to clean up (EPA 2004).

Failing and polluted infrastructure needs to be not simply repaired, but replaced with more advanced, environmentally responsible, cost effective, and sustainable systems that promote conservation of nonrenewable resources. Communities' capability to undertake such infrastructure improvements is becoming more limited. The economic recession of the past four years has significantly reduced the amount of federal, state, and local fiscal resources available for infrastructure investments. Along with this fiscal reality, factors contributing to a huge demand for new, effective and economical methods and materials include: increasing population growth; voter opposition to infrastructure projects; continual terrorist threats on critical infrastructure; burgeoning government budget deficits; increasing government regulations; environmental design concerns; and skyrocketing energy, labor, and materials costs.

Reshaping Our Communities

Predictions are for the volume of development during the next 30 years in the United States to exceed any previous period (Nelson 2004). By 2030, growth-related and replacement development will be more than two-thirds of all development. About half of the buildings in which Americans live, work, and shop will have been built since 2000, with an estimated $25 trillion invested.

Historically, federal, state, and local governmental policy, spending programs, school integration, and tax expenditures have fundamentally shaped growth in metropolitan areas of the United States. These policies traditionally have facilitated decentralization of urban areas and provided financial barriers and impediments to redevelopment and reinvestment (Katz 2002). Current patterns of low-density residential development also are the most expensive to serve with infrastructure, (estimated to be $90,000 per one-acre lot versus $130,000 per five-acre lot). Continuing to promote low-density sprawl will cause communities greater fiscal distress than pursuing more moderate-density development (Burchell et al. 2002).

Research suggests that growth management leading to higher-density development patterns saves communities money and improves prospects for economic development (Cervero 2000; Muro and Puentes 2004; Nelson and Peterman 2000). Researchers predict that less than half of predicted new development will be in conventional sprawl (Nelson 2004). Instead, pressure will be put on many central cities, suburbs, and second-tier suburbs with large amounts of vacant, under-utilized land. Redevelopment also will prevail as buildings are designed for shorter and shorter life spans. The U.S. Department of Energy reports that the average age of buildings devoted to food sales is 19.5 years, and for retail space other than enclosed malls it is 24.5 years (Energy Information Agency 2002). It is predicted that between 2000 and 2030, all of the existing 6 billion square feet devoted to these two building types will be replaced, some twice (Nelson 2004).

Restoring Our Resources

Current rates of resource consumption related to construction and land development are unsustainable. Construction activities worldwide consume 3 billion tons of raw materials each year, or 40 percent of total global use (Roodman and Lenssen 1995). Buildings in the United States account for 65 percent of electricity consumption, 36 percent of total energy use, 30 percent of greenhouse-gas emissions, 30 percent of water and materials consumption, and generate similar proportions of pollution (The Economist 2004).

Meeting current and future restoration demands will require not only conservation of nonrenewable resources, but also development of new, more advanced, resource-responsible, and cost-effective materials, manufacturing, and construction processes. Considerable advances have been made in the development of advanced materials, fabrication, and component assembly of automobiles, ships, and airplanes. The potential currently exists for adaptation of these materials and methods for construction of buildings (Kieran and Timberlake 2004) and other urban infrastructure, including utility and digital systems.

Restoring Our Minds and Bodies

Current automobile-dependent land use patterns in the United States have contributed to the inactivity, obesity, and associated diseases that now are emerging as major public health challenges. In 1996, the Natural Resource Defense Council estimated that 64,000 people die prematurely each year due to air pollution exposure. Vehicular and industrial emissions threaten public health by increasing the risk of respiratory and cardiovascular disease and cancer, as well as contribute to global warming (Shprentz, Bryner, and Shprentz 1996).

A clear relationship has been established between negative design qualities such as the degree of sprawl, lack of security in public spaces, limited transportation alternatives, and undesirable community design characteristics and such adverse health effects as reduced walking; increased rates of hypertension, diabetes, and coronary heart disease; body weight; and the probability of being obese (Frumkin, Frank, and Jackson 2004). Transportation research has long shown that higher-density, mixed land use development is associated with more walking and fewer health problems.

Between 2000 and 2030, the number of people ages 65 and over will more than double (U.S. Census Bureau 2000). Such a demographic shift toward an aging population is predicted to double the number of elderly oriented housing to 70 million units, making it the fastest growing segment of the housing market. The aging population also will drive increased interest in tourism and recreation after 2010, when the leading edge of the Baby Boom generation reaches retirement age. This demographic group is driving a shift in tourism from a primary demand for commercial attractions toward a new interest in authentic experiences as they seek more rewarding ways to spend their time and money (Gardner 2005; Martin, McGuire, and Allen 1998). Visitors increasingly are attracted to experiential recreation and places with a distinctive personality and character, such as small towns, historic sites, working farms, scenic byways, biking and hiking trails, and nature preserves.

Reshaping Our Economies

The world economy has changed in fundamental ways since World War II. The economy of the United States is no longer the single dominant economy (Drucker 2005). The emerging economy is comprised predominantly of a number of economic blocs and, to a lesser extent, individual national-states. Drucker names six or seven blocs, including the U.S.-dominated North American Free Trade Agreement, the European Union, MERCOSUR in Latin America, ASEAN in the Far East, and nation-states that are blocs themselves, such as China and India (Drucker 2005).

The world's economic blocs increasingly are comprised of multinational companies – growing from 7,258 in 1969 to 63,000 by 2000 and accounting for more than 80 percent of the world's industrial production (Drucker 2005). The companies are organized by markets – not geography – with less than 40 percent of the world's 500 largest multinationals headquartered in the United States (185 are in the United States, 126 in the European Union, and 108 in Japan). These multinationals are domestic companies with foreign *partners*, not foreign *subsidiaries*.

The new world economy is forcing the U.S. economy to undergo significant infrastructural change. Communities large and small are finding it difficult to compete in the new global, knowledge-based economy. Many communities are inhibited by a mix of existing slow-growth industries and a poor-quality economic infrastructure, characterized by lack of access to a skilled work force, research and development, transportation, financing, and information technology.

Michael Porter asserts that the most successful economic development strategies steer away from a traditional government policy–driven model focused on short term incentives such as tax rebates or low-cost facilities. The more successful strategies use a collaborative, cluster model centered on a network of leading firms, government, educational institutions, and access to technology, suppliers, talented workforce pool, and the state's regulatory environment (DRI•WEFA Inc. 2002). The synergistic effect of a cluster of similar companies in one region renders individual companies more competitive, adaptable, and productive. Traditional community economic development strategies place primary emphasis on the generation of new technology versus distribution, accessibility, and the application of technology (DRI•WEFA Inc. 2002). Learning, the flow of intellectual resources, and the ability of the network members to recombine existing knowledge into new skills, technologies, and services is the central economic activity of the cluster. Clusters are reported to produce more jobs and are essential to attracting additional competitive and innovative companies to a region.

Well-known clusters include the automotive cluster in Detroit, entertainment industry in Hollywood, and information technology industry in Silicon Valley. The Research Triangle cluster in North Carolina and the laser optics cluster in Arizona are examples of clusters that grew out of a strategic approach to the creation of a cluster. Cluster analysis has been a key component of formulating economic development strategy in other states as well, including Colorado, Connecticut, Florida, Georgia, Iowa, Louisiana, Massachusetts, Minnesota, Mississippi, Missouri, New Mexico, New York, North Dakota, Oregon, Pennsylvania, Tennessee, Virginia, and Utah (Porter and Monitor Company Group 2003). European industrial cluster policies have been in use for many years, and cluster analysis is driving the formation of cluster groups in Sri Lanka, Mexico, Australia, Canada, and Singapore. The United States must strengthen regional clusters of innovation to remain competitive in such a global setting (The Council on Competitiveness 2001).

As manufacturing and technology-related services continue to move and/or outsource overseas, local economies must look more to their inherent assets and develop strategies to position these resources more advantageously. Ironically, the depressed economies of many rural and small towns in the United States may have preserved and left intact the very resources that may now serve as engines of future economic growth. Under this new paradigm, strategies for the protection and enhancement of historic, natural, and cultural resources and revitalization of small towns have become critical potential components of an economic development cluster (Gardner 2005).

Restoration Challenges in South Carolina

Like many areas in the southern United States, the restoration challenges in the state of South Carolina are significant. South Carolina is predicted to grow by one million people by 2020, with one-third on the coast. The American Association of Retired Persons lists South Carolina as the second fastest-growing state in the South in terms of in-migrant retirees, and in the top seven retirement locations in the nation (Allen 2002). South Carolina places seventh in the nation in commercial and institutional square feet demand ranked by the percentage of square feet predicted to be built between 2000 and 2030 (Nelson 2004).

The Greenville/Spartanburg area has been ranked as the fifth most sprawling metropolitan region in the United States, just behind metro-Atlanta (Urban Land Institute/South Carolina Real Estate Center South Carolina Quality Growth Initiative 2004). South Carolina's growth is predicted to require 743,000 new housing units; 64 million square feet of retail space; 66 million square feet of industrial buildings; 23,000 hotel rooms; and $57 billion in infrastructure costs largely to be borne by local, state, and federal governments (Urban Land Institute/South Carolina Real Estate Center South Carolina Quality Growth Initiative 2004).

South Carolina is not able to maintain its current urban infrastructure, let alone accommodate such significant growth. According to the Environmental Protection Agency, South Carolina must invest $1.7 billion over the next 20 years to repair state's existing sewer systems (EPA 1996). Of this amount, an estimated $840 million is needed for treatment technologies and $820 million to upgrade the state's drinking water facilities. Twenty-two percent of South Carolina's major roads are in poor or mediocre condition (ASCE 2005b), 23 percent of bridges are structurally deficient or functionally obsolete, and 39 percent of urban freeways are congested. Sixty-six percent of South Carolina schools have at least one unsatisfactory environmental condition. One in five South Carolinians live in manufactured and mobile homes, which constitute 20 percent of all housing in the state (South Carolina State Housing Finance and Development Authority 2003).

South Carolina also faces significant air and water quality and quantity issues. Vehicle travel on highways in South Carolina increased by 40 percent from 1991 to 2003 while the state's population grew by only 19 percent during that same period (ASCE 2005b). Several regions in South Carolina face the serious risk of failing to meet federal ozone standards established under the U.S. Clean Air Act. Clean water is growing scarcer as demand increases. Twenty-four percent of South Carolina's adult population is obese, with high rates of diabetes (Centers for Disease Control and Prevention 2002).

Several barriers currently prevent South Carolina and its communities from dealing with restoration and growth challenges that require the work of interdisciplinary restoration-related research teams. They include: lack of a state framework to encourage planning and investment for quality growth and development; lack of interjurisdictional coordination caused by fiscal disincentives and conflicting political and policy objectives; state and local regulatory practices that encourage single-use, low-density, environmentally detrimental development; uncoordinated or insufficient funding for transportation and other infrastructure; lack of affordable housing options; and a failure to adequately protect key environmental resources (Urban Land Institute/South Carolina Real Estate Center South Carolina Quality Growth Initiative 2004).

Economic Challenges in South Carolina

South Carolina's economy is undergoing considerable transition. Portions of the state are experiencing extraordinary growth and development while others languish. For example, the state's Upstate region boasts the highest international investment per capita in the United States, with more than 215 international firms (Upstate Alliance 2005) while unemployment rates in the Pee Dee region remain well above the national average. South Carolina will not be able to compete in the new, knowledge-based economy despite a relative advantage in labor costs and taxation if it continues to rely on the traditional mix of industries and to lack a quality economic foundation (DRI•WEFA Inc. 2002).

Existing economic clusters in South Carolina are concentrated in slow-growing industries (basic materials, textiles, and automotive assembly) that have not yet established a coordinated development strategy. The most diverse and promising clusters are transportation equipment, advanced materials, and components and sub-assemblies (DRI•WEFA Inc. 2002). Dubbed the "New Southern Motown," the Greenville/Spartanburg area is home to BMW North America and a Michelin production facility, along with some 200 related suppliers. The chemicals, plastics, glass, and rubber industries are strongly linked to other clusters in South Carolina and are spinning off multiple seed companies. Although it is smaller than the other clusters the components and sub-assemblies cluster is predicted to have the fastest growth over the next five years. The advanced materials seed cluster is the most diverse, with nearly 50 companies producing advanced textile composites, polyolefin products, specialized chemical compounds and products, and ceramic composite products.

Porter recommends that to succeed, South Carolina should develop a coordinated cluster initiative that diversifies industry and strengthens the existing economic infrastructure (DRI•WEFA Inc. 2002). Porter's cluster analysis reveals that South Carolina's business environment is challenged by the limited supply of advanced degree holders, first-tier research universities, scientists and engineers, skilled workers, and technicians; relatively weak K–12 and advanced educational systems; limited coordination between universities and companies; few cluster-specific institutions for collaboration; few statewide organizations working to upgrade the quality of all elements of the business environment; and incentives and attention skewed to attracting large outside firms to the state (Porter and Monitor Company Group 2003). Conversely, South Carolina benefits from low wages, taxes, rent, and utilities; a flexible, hard-working labor force; high quality of life along some dimensions; good transportation infrastructure: seaport and interstates; responsive, high quality technical colleges; and proximity to assets in Georgia and North Carolina.

The Porter analysis further identifies potential technology-based seed clusters (Table 1) (DRI•WEFA Inc. 2002). These technology assets generally consist of public and private research and development establishments.

Finally, Porter makes the following recommendations regarding the development of a cluster industry strategy for South Carolina (Porter and Monitor Company Group 2003):

1.   Foster connectivity between clusters to drive economic performance.

2.   Capitalize on research and development conducted in the state, both govern-ment-sponsored and corporate initiatives.

3.   Establish industry partnerships between colleges and universities. Create a networking organization in each research university to align research with lo-cal firms' interests and capabilities.

4.   Encourage research and development in the state by offering tax incentives to companies for research conducted in the state, and raise the reward if it is conducted in the state in conjunction with a local university.

5.   Coordinate higher education priorities statewide and improve the quality and standards of colleges and universities, with some institutions focusing on train-ing that specifically correlates to industry clusters and workforce requirements needed within the state.

6.   Develop a more comprehensive endowed-chair program to attract top academics to teach at colleges and universities.

7.   Market South Carolina's quality of life and relatively low taxes as a major incentive for recruiting knowledge-based businesses and encourag-ing expansions. In tandem with possible tourism cluster initiatives, focus on broadening the state's array of cultural and recreational opportuni-ties.

Restoration Economy Opportunities in South Carolina

While South Carolina faces daunting growth and infrastructure challenges, it also enjoys the prospect of turning such challenges into a significant opportunity. By forming a restoration related technology and services related cluster around university research expertise, related business and industry, and state and municipal government, South Carolina can become an international leader

Table 1. Technology-Based Seed Clusters
Apparel
Components and Sub-Assemblies
Food and Agriculture
Forestry, Wood, and Paper
Machinery and Fabricated Metals
Materials
Professional Services
Textiles
Tourism
Transportation Services and Equipment
Advanced Materials
Software, Hardware, and Internet
Nanotechnology
Environmental Science
Horticulture and Related
Defense and Related
Pharmaceuticals
Source: DRI•WEFA Inc. 2002

in the generation of new restoration knowledge. This knowledge capital can be used to meet not only the restoration needs of South Carolina, but also constitutes valuable capital and infrastructure for a national cluster specializing in restoration much in the same way as the automotive cluster in Detroit and the laser optics cluster in Arizona. Potential cluster industries identified by Porter that are also related to restoration development include those listed in Table 2.

South Carolina's wealth of distinctive historic and natural assets, including its climate, coastline, and mountains, makes retirement and resort communities, tourism, and recreation the most dominant sectors of the state's economy, totaling $6.3 billion annually (South Carolina Budget and Control Board 2005). The Palmetto Institute has ranked South Carolina fifth nationally in the Cluster Power Index for tourism, and predicts that the tourism market will experience very rapid growth over the next five years (DRI•WEFA Inc., 2002). The estimated value of South Carolina's real estate is $450 trillion. Growth predictions for the next 20 years will have both positive and negative impacts on this value. Accommodating growth while preserving, restoring, and conserving South Carolina's unique historic, cultural, and natural resources is vitally important to local communities and to the economic health of the entire state.

In the new restoration economy, local economies in South Carolina communities must look to position its inherent assets more strategically in order to expand the tourism industry even further (Gardner 2005). As was the case with Charleston, rural and small town economies must leverage historic, cultural, and natural resources as engines of future economic growth. Restoration-related research focused on the protection and enhancement of historic, natural, and cultural resources and revitalization of small towns is critical to South Carolina's economic development. To realize its potential, the state needs more specialized tourism research centers to conduct market research, greater support for specialized education and training programs, and a policy framework and catalyzing collaborative efforts (Porter 2003).

Porter and The South Carolina Council on

Table 2. Potential Restoration-Related Seed Clusters
Components and Sub-Assemblies
Food and Agriculture
Forestry, Wood, and Paper
Machinery and Fabricated Metals
Materials
Professional Services
Textiles
Tourism
Transportation Equipment
Transportation Services
Advanced Materials
Software, Hardware, and Internet
Nanotechnology (materials and electronic)
Environmental Science
Horticulture and Related
Defense and Related
Source: DRI•WEFA Inc. 2002

Competitiveness identify other potential restoration-related industry cluster opportunities, including tourism, advanced material science, biochemistry, environmental science/engineering, transportation equipment and services, and heavy construction services (DRI•WEFA Inc., 2002). there is a strong demand for regional coordination and planning of cost-effective and sustainable solutions to the growth challenges facing South Carolina and communities throughout the country and world. Industrial manufacturing could help support the development of an environmental and infrastructure restoration technologies cluster, together with the technology assets in the state, which can link back to other manufacturing industries such as wood and paper products as well as the specialized professional restoration services cluster.

The Clemson University Restoration Institute

To help meet the restoration development needs of South Carolina and the United States as a whole, Clemson University established the Restoration Institute in 2004. The Institute's mission is to advance knowledge in integrative approaches to the restoration of historic, ecological, and urban infrastructure resources. The Institute drives economic growth through the creation, development, and production of restoration industries and technology; patented advanced materials; cost-efficient and environmentally sensitive land development practices and policies; and the development and renewal of restoration-related professional disciplines and highly trained workforces.

Through its design and planning studios and research laboratories at Clemson University and in the Lowcountry of South Carolina, the Institute provides hands-on research and educational opportunities for undergraduate and graduate students through internships and industrial fellowships. The Institute is attracting world-renowned faculty, students, and staff in various areas of restoration development to create a leading knowledge-based, export-oriented industry cluster that will position Clemson University and the South Carolina's Lowcountry as international leaders in restoration knowledge and expertise.

The Restoration Institute has received support from the state of South Carolina and the cities of Charleston and North Charleston. The Institute was selected by the state as a South Carolina Center for Economic Excellence and given a pledge of matching monies for an endowed professorship in materials conservation. The Institute is pursuing three additional endowed chairs, one each in urban ecology, advanced materials, and health care design. In addition, it is pursing support via the South Carolina Research University Infrastructure Act that was enacted to facilitate and increase research at the state's research universities through research infrastructure projects. The act provides state funds to match non-state capital to enable the three state research universities to construct or support facilities and acquire research equipment. that the facilities and equipment will, in turn, help universities recruit and retain high-caliber faculty and students and successfully compete for public and private research funding. Eligible projects include single buildings; clusters of buildings; geographic areas set aside for development of research facilities such as a research campus, laboratories, equipment, or office space; and infrastructure improvements.

Under the leadership of Mayor Joseph P. Riley, the City of Charleston has provided significant support to the Restoration Institute, specifically the Clemson Architecture Center in Charleston, through a gift of land for the construction of the new Architecture Center facility. Similarly, Clemson University is engaged in discussions with the City of North Charleston concerning the acquisition of land on the location of a former Naval Base for the possible development of a restoration-related technology transfer campus.

Partnerships with state and municipal governments are critical to the technology transfer process and the creation of incubator businesses. Clemson University and the economic development arms of the State of South Carolina and the cities of Charleston and North Charleston are working together to advance each required step of technology transfer and business development – research, product development, capital generation, marketing, and management.

Restoration Institute Teams

The Clemson University Restoration Institute is in its initial stages of development. The Institute's work is conducted by interdisciplinary teams of faculty, research staff, and students. The Institute works collaboratively with business, industry, government agencies, and nonprofit organizations to transfer knowledge to established and future incubator businesses, industries, and professions and advance the creation of a restoration cluster in South Carolina. Restoration teams have four areas of focus: 1) Preservation and Conservation, 2) Advanced Materials and Methods, 3) Urban Ecology, and 4) Healthy Communities and Buildings.

Restoration teams research the restoration and reconstruction of sustainable and healthy environments in deteriorated urban areas, impacted waterways, abandoned industrial areas, natural and human-made disaster areas, and suburban or rural areas under pressures of sprawl. Team members develop new strategies, technology, and materials for infrastructure improvement, both built and natural, by pioneering collaborative work among disciplines that do not traditionally interact. Special emphasis is placed on the interstitial areas between established disciplines and the new knowledge that results from such collaborative research. The outcome is innovative strategies, technology, and tools to solve environmental problems that contribute to high urban infrastructure costs, economic decline, and health problems in towns and cities.

The Preservation and Conservation Team conducts research in the areas of historic preservation, tourism, and materials conservation. The scale of work ranges considerably from the macro – documentation and preservation of large-scale historic landscapes and cityscapes and development of integrated preservation-oriented land development and tourism practices, policies, and financing strategies – to the micro – methods of conservation and cyclical maintenance of historic buildings, structures, and gardens and discovery and testing of methods for stabilization and curation of cloth, masonry, wood, and iron artifacts.

This team draws from the fields of historic preservation, architecture, landscape architecture, city and regional planning, real estate development, tourism, history, art history, communication studies, environmental ethics, literature, religion, geography, visual arts, materials conservation and sciences, building pathology, construction science, and digital production arts. The centerpiece of the team is Clemson University's newly initiated Master of Science in Historic Preservation and Master of Real Estate Development degrees.

The Advanced Materials and Methods Team conducts research in next-generation materials that enable more efficient and environment-friendly structures (merged ceramics, polymers, biomaterials and composites, fibrous protein materials and high thermal conductivity carbon fibers); design processes (supercomputing-based, biomimetic process and product development and modeling utilizing interfacial biophysics, surface engineering, and virtual rendering of structures); and new fabrication and assembly processes (integrated systems combining mechanical, electrical, fiber optic, and digital technologies and process manufacturing and component assembly technologies).

This team adapts research at the Clemson University International Center for Automotive Research and Center for Advanced Engineering Fibers and Films to building construction. Disciplines involved include materials sciences and engineering; molecular biology; bio- and genetic engineering; mathematics; photonics; industrial, electrical, mechanical, and civil engineering; real estate development; forestry; hydrology; city and regional planning; architecture; landscape architecture; construction science and management; environmental ethics; and digital production arts.

The Urban Ecology Team conducts research in the areas of land development and management and the restoration of ecological systems. Team research is focused on soil systems (contaminated soil remediation), water systems (river, stream, wetland, estuaries, bays, and coastline ecosystem and storm and wastewater management), and urban forest and wildlife habitat regeneration and management.

This team combines the disciplines of basic ecological science, environmental and biosystems engineering, hydrology, environmental toxicology, urban forestry management, fisheries and wildlife management, landscape architecture, city and regional planning, real estate development, environmental ethics, history, and geography. Clemson's newly initiated Ph.D. in Urban Design and Planning supports the team's work. A proposed endowed professorship in Urban Ecology, which is under consideration by the South Carolina Commission on Higher Education for matching funds, will conduct the scholarship and research necessary for the integration of basic ecological science with engineering, urban design, and planning.

The Healthy Communities and Buildings Team conducts research in the design, planning, and management of communities for healthy living. The work's scale ranges from the regional (planned integration of watersheds, urban forests, multi-modal transportation systems, and other land uses for air and water quality) to the community (planning and design of walkable and safe neighborhoods) to the site (design of "green" health care facilities and therapeutic landscapes and gardens) to the building (design and construction of healthy buildings with maximum natural daylighting and interior products and finishes with zero toxic emissions).

This team combines the disciplines of pathology, nursing, public health, gerontology, toxicology, architecture, landscape architecture, construction science and management, civil and environmental engineering, city and regional planning, real estate development, economics, public policy, horticulture, education, environmental ethics, communication studies, geography, history, foreign languages, psychology, sociology, and performing arts. Clemson architecture faculty are collaborating with the Medical University of South Carolina in Charleston and Berchtold Corporation to conduct research on the design of safe and effective surgical care facilities.

The Lowcountry of South Carolina – The Restoration Laboratory

The Lowcountry of South Carolina provides an ideal laboratory for the Clemson University Restoration Institute. The Lowcountry is the area consisting of the entire lower coastal plane of South Carolina. The combination of restoration-related challenges located within one region – the nation's largest and most well-preserved historic city (Charleston), second largest active Atlantic port (Charleston), largest remaining protected undeveloped coastal wetland ecosystems (ACE Basin), one of the fastest-growing and most sprawling metropolitan regions (Beaufort/Bluffton area), and the largest urban infill project in the country (North Charleston-Noisette) – presents an unparalleled, real-life laboratory for restoration research and teaching.

The Lowcountry is a rich network of barrier islands, saltwater marshes, blackwater and bald cypress swamps, tidal rivers, abandoned rice fields and plantations, historic towns and cities, ports and industrial areas, and residential resort and retirement communities. The earliest evidence of human habitation, shellfish middens, indicates that humans have inhabited the South Carolina Lowcountry for more than 12,000 years. Originally home to a number of Native American tribes, the land was settled by the English, French Huguenots, and Africans. From the early 1700s to the mid 1800s, tens of thousands of acres of bottomland hardwoods along the navigable rivers and creeks of the area were converted to rice fields (McCrady 1897). During this period, some 80 large plantations, owned by a small number of individuals, generated enormous wealth. The South Carolina Lowcountry was the wealthiest region in the mainland British North America on the eve of the American Revolution in 1776 (Linder 1995).

The English and French utilized Dutch engineers to supervise projects and West African slave labor and knowledge of rice cultivation and swamp culture to construct and manage the fields. Without this large, inexpensive labor force, the irrigation system and cultivation of the marsh landscape would have been impossible. The extensive network of banks, canals, and ditches changed the natural landscape dramatically. Many rice fields are still visible today in aerial photographs. After it was harvested, rice was ferried on barges and schooners to the burgeoning ports in Charleston and Beaufort. At the height of the industry, the plantations produced 95 percent of the nation's rice (Linder 1995). The rice was called "Carolina Gold," a variety named for the color of its outer hull. It was considered the best-quality rice in the world.

The emancipation of slaves in 1864, industrial advancements, and the hurricanes of 1910 and 1911 brought the slow decline and eventual demise of the rice culture in South Carolina. In the late 19th and early 20th centuries, most rice planters sold out to timber companies or to wealthy northern capitalists who used the rice fields as hunting preserves. The resultant development of sophisticated wildlife management techniques led to the effective preservation of the Lowcountry's indigenous landscape and cultural character.

Charleston Historic Peninsula –
Conserving and Restoring a Contemporary Historic City

Another important aspect of the Lowcountry is its historic cities. Charleston's historic architecture, building craft, garden architecture, and cultural landscapes arguably are among the most significant in North America. From the late 1700s through the mid 1800s, Charleston was a center for processing and selling rice as well as the center of business and social life for rice planters. The poverty that descended on the city following the Civil War persisted well into the 20th century and had the unintended effect of preserving much of the historic city. Ironically, the poor economic conditions allowed Charleston to be bypassed by much of the urban renewal movement in the United States from the 1930s through the 1960s, thus preserving much of the historic city from demolition.

In addition to the establishment of one of the first preservation societies in the country in the 1920s and 1930s, Charleston was the first city to adopt zoning ordinances to promote historic districts as well as to preserve and integrate historic buildings into the plan for a public housing complex. From the beginning of the 20th century, and more recently under the leadership of Mayor Joseph P. Riley, Charleston has become an international leader in urban design, redevelopment, and historic preservation. Such success has not been without significant challenges, however – population growth and sprawl threaten the very livability and environmental quality central to this success.

Charleston is the home of the Clemson University Graduate Program in Historic Preservation and the Clemson University Architecture Center in Charleston. The Historic Preservation Program is multidisciplinary, integrating design, planning, engineering, and science professions with the humanities for teaching and research in historic preservation and cultural resource management. The program's focus is preservation planning and design, management, and conservation and interpretation of historic and cultural structures, gardens, districts, and landscapes.

An international design competition has been completed for a new architecture center facilty on the historic peninsula on land donated by the City of Charleston. Construction was scheduled to begin in early 2006. The first LEED-certified building in Charleston, the center will be the keystone, headquarters facility of the restoration institute in Charleston and will provide offices and studio space for faculty and students of the Clemson University Restoration Institute.

North Charleston –
Integrative Urban and Industrial Site Restoration

A much younger municipality by historic Charleston standards, the city of North Charleston provides a contrasting restoration laboratory. Mostly traders, ship builders and farmers, the first European colonists arrived in North Charleston in the 1600's. The area experienced repeated boom-and-bust cycles as it transitioned from agrarian land use to military/industrial uses. After the park board commissioned the Olmsted brothers to design a large garden, Chicora Park, in 1898, wealthy Charlestonians sought out the area as a tourist destination.

North Charleston, incorporated in 1972, is the site of the former Charleston Navy Base, which for 100 years was one of the nation's largest and most active military bases. The base was closed in the mid 1990s as part of a federal military reorganization, leaving a large inventory of land, vacant buildings, other facilities, and open space centrally located in one of the nation's fastest-growing urban areas. The Port of Charleston remains the second largest active port on the Atlantic Coast.

A major redevelopment project, Noisette, is being undertaken in North Charleston. The $1 billion project encompasses 3,000 acres of the city and former naval base, constituting one of the largest single urban redevelopment projects in the United States. Led by a unique public-private partnership, the Noisette plan seeks to preserve historic architectural styles, neighborhood diversity, and the area's unique social fabric. It also looks to restore environmental stability and beauty, attract jobs, improve services like education and healthcare, reduce dependence on car travel, promote recreation, eliminate the foundations of crime and poverty, and strengthen the sense of pride that many North Charleston residents feel toward their community (Noisette Company 2004).

ACE Basin of South Carolina –
Restoration and Preservation of Pristine Ecosystems

One particular area in the Lowcountry that remains relatively undeveloped is the ACE Basin. The ACE Basin presents as an ecological restoration research laboratory, one of the largest undeveloped wetland estuary ecosystems remaining on the Atlantic coast. Located 45 minutes south of Charleston, the Basin is named for the Ashepoo, Combahee, and Edisto rivers, which meet at South Carolina's biologically rich St. Helena Sound. The Basin region consists of tidal saltwater and brackish-water marshes, maritime forests, upland pines, bottomland hardwoods, old rice fields, and historic plantation homes.

Because of its remoteness, relatively pristine nature, and extensive, diverse habitats, the ACE Basin provides an ideal restoration laboratory for interdisciplinary research in biological diversity, pollution impact assessment on the structure and function of ecosystems, and sustainable production systems. In addition, the ACE Basin provides a framework for comparative studies of similar problems in different coastal regions.

The Basin's three major rivers in the ACE Basin each have extensive drainage areas. The Edisto, with 250 miles of unobstructed river and extensive watershed, is one of the longest free-flowing blackwater rivers in the United States. The combination of six distinct ecosystem habitat-types provide a home for 1,500 different plant and animal species, including federally designated endangered species such as the shortnose sturgeon, wood storks, West Indian manatee, loggerhead sea turtles, and bald eagles (Heritage Trust Database 1997). The ACE Basin area is primarily rural, with only five incorporated communities. The main land use types in the Basin are agriculture, acquaculture, and silviculture with secondary uses for hunting, commercial and recreational fishing, hiking, kayaking, and tourism.

Formal protection of the ACE Basin began in 1988 with the creation of the ACE Basin Task Force, a nationally and internationally recognized partnership of state and federal governmental representatives, nonprofit conservation organizations, and private landowners. The U.S. Fish and Wildlife Service, South Carolina Department of Natural Resources, Ducks Unlimited, The Nature Conservancy, Colleton County, and private landowners have joined in an effort to preserve and enhance the 350,000-acre ACE Basin area (ACE Basin Website 2005). The private landowner initiative has been fundamental to the ACE Basin Project's overwhelming success. The ACE Basin National Estuarine Research Reserve and Wildlife Refuge is part of the ACE Basin Project, a flagship project of the North American Waterfowl Management Plan.

To date, well over 128,000 acres have been protected through conservation easements, management agreements, and fee title purchases. The management goal has been to maintain the unique character of the Basin region, including traditional land uses such as agriculture, timber production, hunting, and fishing, while limiting industrial and resort development characteristic of much of the state's coastal zone in the past 30 years (ACE Basin Project 2005).

Several factors threaten the Basin's future, as well as the entire South Carolina Low-country environment, the primary ones being environmental and socioeconomic problems associated with rapid urbanization of the region (ACE Basin Economic Forum 1996). A popular second home and retirement location, the population of the ACE Basin study area is expected to increase by 30 percent between 1990 and 2010. In 1990, nearly one-quarter of the Basin area's population lived in poverty (MRRI/NOAA ACE Basin 1998), in contrast to wealthier resort and high-end residential community residents. The lack of job opportunities in the ACE River Basin drives nearly a third of its residents to travel to work outside the area (U.S. Census Bureau 1990), making the Basin area a bedroom community for the cities of Charleston and Beaufort. One of the greatest threats to habitat diversity in the ACE Basin is the conversion of existing habitats to biologically simpler habitats such as agricultural fields, pine plantations, and urban or residential areas, with the resulting fragmentation of the remaining forested and wetland areas (Beasley et al. 1996).

With growth comes increased water use. Water quality in the ACE Basin faces many challenges, including saltwater encroachment into groundwater aquifers because of high water use by Hilton Head and Savannah; bio- and chemical pollution caused by runoff from urban, industrial, timber harvesting, and agricultural activities; turbidity and sedimentation due to urban land use, boating, beachfront modifications, and dredging or filling of channels and wetlands (Alexander and Wenner 1995); and human and animal pathogens, including fecal coliform. Such problems often require frequent closure of shellfish beds. The South Carolina Department of Health and Environmental Control also has issued fish consumption advisories for parts of the ACE Basin due to mercury levels.

The Clemson University Restoration Institute conducts research in the Basin region, focusing on the development of effective land use planning and watershed-based zoning policy and regulations. Such policy and regulations seek to reduce water consumption to control impervious surface coverage, to reduce chemical contaminants in point source and nonpoint source runoff, and to prevent pollution from entering aquatic systems. The Institute works with local governments and state and federal agencies to develop an effective system of comprehensive planning for conservation land use, stormwater control, enhanced treatment of effluents, and best management practices for forestry and agriculture.

Our Future Restored and Transformed

The most successful cities and metropolitan regions of the future will be those that best meet the immense and complex challenges of human-made and natural infrastructure restoration. Success will require application of new strategies, materials, and methods for restoration. Communities should establish knowledge clusters around cooperating governmental and nongovernmental agencies, universities, and business and industry that are dedicated to restoration related-research. The communities that are equipped to do that will be best positioned to meet local and regional restoration challenges and to export such knowledge nationally and internationally. The Clemson University Restoration Institute, its various partners, and Lowcountry laboratories represent the first such emerging knowledge cluster in the United States. Through graduate education, research, and outreach the Restoration Institute plays a central role in the transformation and restoration of communities throughout South Carolina, the United States, and the world.

Like the metropolitan regions within which they reside, universities also are undergoing transformation. Universities are required as never before to compete regionally, nationally, and internationally for everything from students and faculty to grants and governmental funding to private gifts and relationships with business and industry. Whether driven by internal or external pressures such as decreasing state and federal support for higher education or increasing demands to serve as economic engines, universities are reinventing their missions and ways of operating. The Restoration Institute is driving a transformation of Clemson University in a number of ways from curricula to promotion and tenure criteria to accreditation standards to organizational structure to the nature of partnerships. Perhaps driven by a different set of factors than in the past, the metropolis and the university are required to cooperate as never before. The success of both the metropolis and the university are inextricably tied.

References

ACE Basin Economic Forum. 1996. ACE Basin Economic Forum: Health Economy, Healthy Environment: An Action Agenda for Compatible Economic Development. Walterboro, SC.

ACE Basin Project Website. 2005. www.walterboro.org/ACE-Basin/passim.

Allen, Jeffrey. 2002. Modeling and Predicting of Future Urban Growth in the Charleston, South Carolina Area. Testimony presented to the U.S. Commission on Ocean Policy. Strom Thurmond Institute of Public and Governmental Affairs, Clemson University. January.

Alexander, C., and E. Wenner. 1995. *Evaluating the Historical Record of Nonpoint Source Pollution in the ACE Basin and Sapelo Island National Estuarine Research Reserves.* Final Report submitted to South Carolina Sea Grant Consortium. South Carolina Department of Natural Resources, Marine Resources Division, Charleston, SC and Skidaway Institute of Oceanography, Sapelo Island, GA.

American Society of Civil Engineers. 2005a. *Progress Report. America's Infrastructure.* Reston, VA: American Society of Civil Engineers

American Society of Civil Engineers. 2005b. *Infrastructure Report Card – South Carolina.* Reston, VA: American Society of Civil Engineers

Beasley, B.R., W.D. Marshall, A.H. Miglarese, J.D. Scurry, and C. Vanden Gouten. 1996. *Managing Resources for a Sustainable Future. The Edisto River Basin Project Report.* Columbia, SC: South Carolina Department of Natural Resources, Water Resources Division.

Burchell, Robert, George Lowenstein, William R. Dolphin, and Catherine C. Galley. 2002. *Costs of Sprawl 2000.* Washington: National Academy Press.

Centers for Disease Control and Prevention. 2002. National Center for Chronic Disease Prevention and Health Promotion, Diabetes Public Health Resource. Prevalence of Diabetes. Available at www.cdc.gov/diabetes/statistics/prev/national/tables8.htm.

Cervero, Robert. 2000. *Efficient Urbanization: Economic Performance and the Shape of the Metropolis*. Working Paper. Lincoln Institute of Land Policy.

Council on Competitiveness. 2001. U.S. Competitiveness 2001: Strengths, Vulnerabilities and Long-Term Priorities. Washington: Council on Competitiveness.

Cunningham, Storm. 2002. *Restoration Economy. The Greatest New Frontier. Immediate and Emerging Opportunities for Businesses, Communities, and Investors.* San Francisco: Berrett-Koehler. DRI•WEFA Inc. 2002. The South Carolina Challenge: Regional Economic Analysis. The Palmetto Institute. Pp. 30–39.

Drucker, Peter. 2005. Trading Places. *Chronicle of Higher Education*, March 17.

The Economist. 2004. The Rise of the Green Building. December 2. Available at www.economist.com/science/tq/displaystory.cfm?story_id=3422965.

Environmental Protection Agency. 1996. *Clean Water Needs Survey*. Washington, DC: Author.

Environmental Protection Agency. 2004. *Cleaning Up the Nation's Waste Sites: Markets and Technology Trends.* Available at www.clu-in.org/market/.

Energy Information Administration. 2002. Commercial Buildings Energy Consumption Survey. Washington, DC: U.S. Department of Energy.
Frumkin, Howard, Lawrence Frank, and Richard Jackson. Urban Sprawl and Public Health. Designing, Planning, and Building Healthy Communities. Island Press. 2004.

Gardner, Edwin. 2005. *Concept Paper: Authentic Experiences – An Emerging Paradigm. A Heritage Area Research and Development Program at Clemson.* Charleston, SC: Heritage Strategy Group.

Heritage Trust Database 1997. List of Threatened and Endangered Species. Columbia, SC: South Carolina Department of Natural Resources, Freshwater Fisheries and Wildlife Diversity Division.

Katz, Bruce. 2002. *Smart Growth: The Future of the American Metropolis*. Washington, DC: Brookings Institution.

Kieran, Stephen and James Timberlake. 2004. *Refabricating Architecture. How Manufacturing Methodologies Are Poised to Transform Building Construction.* New York: McGraw Hill.

Linder, Suzanne C. 1995. *Historical Atlas of the Rice Plantations of the ACE Basin 1860*. S.C. Department of Archives and History for the Archives and History Foundation, Ducks Unlimited, and The Nature Conservancy.

Martin, B.S., F.A McGuire, and L.A. Allen. 1998. Retirees' Attitudes Toward Tourism: Implications for Sustainable Development. *Tourism Analysis* 3: 43–51.

McCrady, E. 1897. *The History of South Carolina Under the Proprietary Government 1670-1719*. New York: Macmillan Company.

Marine Resources Research Institute (MRRI) / National Oceanographic and Atmospheric Administration (NOAA) Ashepoo-Combahee-Edisto (ASE) Basin. 1998. Executive Summary Socioeconomic Assessment. Accessed June 4, 2006 at http://www.dnr.sc.gov/marine/mrri/acechar/essocio.htm

Muro, Mark and Robert Puentes. 2004. *Investing in a Better Future: A Review of the Fiscal and Competitive Advantages of Smarter Growth Development Patterns*. Washington, DC: Brookings Institution.

Nelson, Arthur C. 2004. *Toward a New Metropolis. The Opportunity to Rebuild America*. A Discussion Paper Prepared for The Brookings Institution Metropolitan Policy Program, December. Virginia Polytechnic Institute and State University.

Nelson, Arthur C. and David Peterman. 2000. Does Growth Management Matter: The Effect of Growth Management on Economic Performance. *Journal of Planning Education and Research* 19: 277–285.

The Noisette Company. 2004. Noisette Masterplan, North Charleston, SC.

Porter, Michael and Monitor Company Group L.P. 2003. South Carolina Competitive Initiative. Phase I Presentation. Columbia, SC, December 8, pg. 30.

Roodman, D. M. and N. Lenssen. 1995. *A Building Revolution: How Ecology and Health Concerns are Transforming Construction*. Worldwatch Paper 124, March. Washington, DC: Worldwatch Institute,.

Shprentz, D. S., G. C. Bryner, and J. S. Shprentz. 1996. *Breath-Taking: Premature Mortality Due to Particulate Air Pollution in 239 American Cities*. New York: Natural Resources Defense Council.

South Carolina Budget and Control Board. 2005. South Carolina Statistical Abstract. Office of Research and Statistics.

South Carolina State Housing Finance and Development Authority. 2003. South Carolina Comprehensive Housing Needs Assessment, 2003 Annual Update.

U.S. Census Bureau. 1990. Census of Population.

U.S. Census Bureau. 2000. Census of Population.

Upstate Alliance. 2005. Upstate Highlights. Available at www.upstatealliance.com/ markets.

Urban Land Institute/South Carolina Real Estate Center South Carolina Quality Growth Initiative. 2004. Growing By Choice or By Chance. Columbis, SC: ULI/SCREC.

Water Infrastructure Network. 2005. Clean and Safe Water for the 21st Century: A Renewed Commitment to Water and Wastewater Infrastructure. Washington, DC: Water Infrastructure Network.

Chapter 5
Growing the City Inward: Challenges for Education in Urban Design

Ann Forsyth
Gretchen Nicholls

It is projected that in just 30 years there will be significant changes in the construction and reconstruction of the built environment of the United States. Looking for ways to manage growth over the next three decades, it is tempting to seek big ideas and bold proposals to rebuild the metropolitan landscape. This essay argues, however, that big changes too often are translated solely into proposals for development of big land areas, either through building on greenfields on the urban edge or redeveloping older urban areas after scraping them bare to approximate the greenfield state.

After over a century of suburbanization in the United States, however, cities already occupy large tracts of land. Thus it is crucial to use not just big land area models but also increasingly to fill in the city by building on its leftover, underdeveloped parts. Filling the gaps and reweaving the fabric of the city is a traditional process—one that has created many of the most loved urban areas in the world, but also one that often is overlooked in the search for bold solutions.

Of course there are good reasons that city infill building is not done more frequently: high land prices, additional design and development costs, and lack of community support. It can be done, however, and this essay describes the Corridor Housing Initiative in Minnesota as one example of a program that is using leftover urban spaces. Established by a nonprofit organization, the Center for Neighborhoods, the initiative negotiates placement of high-density, affordable housing in existing built up-areas, working at a site level but with a project explicitly framed in terms of its neighborhood, city, and metropolitan context (Center for Neighborhoods 2005; City of Minneapolis 2005).

Drawing on the experience of the innovative Minneapolis Corridor Housing Initiative, this essay explains the kinds of knowledge required for urban infill rebuilding and sketches out the implications for educating professionals and convening experts to facilitate this kind of process. The process of filling in leftover spaces requires new forms of learning for different sorts of professionals and several scales of communities. For example, preparing urban designers and physical planners for this kind of work means developing their skills in participation and listening—skills that many planners have—but also means giving them a deep appreciation for the realities of markets and design. Designers need to accept solutions that are not unique and recast success at the level of the urban fabric rather than the project level. Teaching approaches in the classroom can include modeling the kinds of participatory interactions and social learning that are needed in neighborhoods and regions (Yabes 2005). Although this is hardly big news, it is rarely done, and there are too few positive examples available.

This essay first examines the "big and bold" approach. It then outlines some issues of competing values and possible opportunities in urban development. In a third section it examines the Corridor Housing Initiative as an example of a strategy of using incremental infill in leftover spaces. Finally, it outlines an educational program that can teach future practitioners to deal with a variety of physical scales but also bridge from vision to implementation, linking the skills of the urban design professions of architecture, landscape architecture, and urban planning. Universities can contribute in ways that go beyond the traditional approach of educating for degrees to include conducting urban research and outreach, convening key stakeholders to consider the futures of regions, and providing learning opportunities that go beyond the traditional course model.

Big and Bold

Nelson (2004) projects that by 2035, half of the built environment in the United States will have been built within the past 30 years. This prospect appears to offer tremendous opportunities for urban designers to think big and challenge what is perceived as conventional wisdom.

In physical planning and urban design, these kinds of opportunities cause great excitement. The possibility of building new landscapes is keenly sought after in professions that value built work. While there have been a limited number of big ideas over the past two centuries of industrialization, the quest and market for big bold ideas has been satisfied by recycling these ideas in slightly modified forms, shaped by the key complaints and concerns of the day. The history of urban design and city planning is a history of these variations on a limited set of ideas (Hall 1988; Ward 2002).

In terms of the location of big and bold solutions, starting from scratch on a greenfield with a big new utopian idea is intellectually appealing to designers in particular, and often easiest for developers who implement those designs because of standardization. From early suburbs of the nineteenth cenury to the Radburn planning of the 1920s and new urbanist villages today, greenfield has been the setting for bold re-imaginings of the city by designers and planners. On the part of developers, new areas have allowed far easier building production, big and bold in terms of scale if not ideas. Redevelopment of existing areas is seldom appealing on a large scale as it involves too little standardization—it is hard to make replicable—although from urban renewal to Hope VI there has been a tradition of redevelopment as a big idea. Very often, however—as was the case with both the urban renewal and Hope VI federal programs—this redevelopment in fact involves scraping a site clean to approximate a large greenfield development.

Conventional development, even in its more idealistic forms, thus is often big development in terms of being mass produced on fairly large sites, zoned in large pieces, conforming to local controls covering relatively large municipalities, or even individually designed but in a way that does not provide a real alternative development form. So if the building boom of the next 30 years follows conventional trends—the conventions of the institutions of the development industry, planning, local control, and even high-style design—it is likely to emphasize big land areas.

This is not necessarily a bad thing. There are many terrific examples of innovative developments that respond to the challenges of large-scale building production (Burby and Weiss 1976; Forsyth 2005). There are, however, many more bad, or at most mundane, large-scale development areas. Many of the big and bold ideas that capture the attention of planners and designers, or that are easy to operationalize on a large development scale, have turned out to be bad ideas. They have had unintended consequences of creating new problems, particularly when implemented with the compromises that are common in development. This opens up the question of whether there is an alternative path that can rebuild the city comprehensively but in small pieces. What kind of form would such a process take, and how can higher education prepare planners, designers, and developers for its challenges?

Values and Opportunities

A discussion of good and bad development, and of a form of education to do better, requires a discussion of values and opportunities. Values are important because they provide criteria for judging success; values also can help to identify opportunity spaces because, although there are thousands of potential arrangements of urban form, the number of plausible opportunities is much smaller.

Looking back at urban form over the past century, it is clear that certain urban designs have become dominant because they can satisfy a variety of values. For example, incremental suburban development—or sprawl—can provide privacy and upward mobility as well as closeness to nature and affordable, high-quality housing. Sprawl development can be both exclusionary and egalitarian. It is also profitable and relatively simple to build and administer. It has a very wide market, willing suppliers, and amenable governments.

Designers of the built environment of the future must consider a variety of stakeholders' interests. For example:
- Consumers want a comfortable and convenient life.
- Government leaders want simple administration, successful political careers, and public services provided at a level consistent with their constituencies' desires.
- Designers and developers want to build, although some want to build more volume while others want to build more interesting designs.
- Many people want to preserve natural resources.

Merely fulfilling the interests of multiple stakeholders does not, however, mean that development is good, or that it works at a large scale. Many urban options that might be fine if implemented infrequently are impractical for wide replication. This is the case with the current dominant development approach, which combines very low density suburbanization with a few compact areas for those who prefer them. This approach meets many needs, but in the end it damages nature and does little to avoid social inequality.

The trick in finding a path forward in the urban development arena seems to be to find an urban form that can satisfy even more interests than currently are being served. At present, there are a number of competing urban visions in play that attempt to appeal to multiple values and interests. They can be characterized as:

- Local democracy: values local control over the built environment and tends to incremental change
- Personal mobility: supports automobile dependence
- Individual housing choice, focusing on the person or at most the household: creates sophisticated housing markets
- Access to natural areas: maintains access to open space
- Creating a sense of place: features intricate and memorable design
- Compactness,and sustainability, with social inclusion—somewhat common in big plans but rarely implemented in the United States

The visions at the top of the list are easier to implement because they can be done in small increments, address many interests at one time, and have become the standard way of operating, so they do not meet resistance in the development process. Of course, they rely on some big initial steps—creating local governments and developing transportation infrastructure—but once done, they are easily repeated on new land on the urban edge or in small infill that does not break the pattern of the market.

While prevalent, however, such development patterns don't necessarily solve the problem of how to build the massive number of housing units that will be needed in the next 30 years. It will be hard to remain efficient, respect nature, and maintain a sense of place with standardized outward growth. The United States needs alternatives that can deal with the difficult work of building within the existing urban area.

The Corridor Housing Initiative is one attempt to meet future housing demand in a way that reflects the needs, values, and interests of a variety of groups—local residents, newcomers, local and regional governments, and for-profit and nonprofit developers. It also attempts to mediate between scales of interest: the region, municipality, neighborhood, and individuals. Although a single case, it highlights the potential and challenges of alternative development patterns that mend the fragmented metropolis rather than extend it or replace large portions. It provides a starting point for imagining the kinds of skills, aptitudes, and knowledge that a new form of urban education should provide. It also suggests how off-campus settings could support such educational programs.

Corridor Housing Initiative

The Corridor Housing Initiative (CHI) in Minneapolis, established in 2003, is an innovative program to place higher-density and affordable housing along transit corridors. Work on the five corridors in Phase 1 of the project was completed in 2004 and a second phase started in 2005, expanding to neighboring St. Paul and suburban areas. Siting affordable housing is a problem throughout the country, and the initiative provides one model for partnering with neighborhoods to fulfill their needs as well as the demand for housing.

Coordinated by the Center for Neighborhoods, and in collaboration with the City of Minneapolis, the CHI emerged as a partnership among Minneapolis neighborhoods, developers, and local governments that connects market opportunities with neighborhood goals. Focusing on proactive planning, partnership, and production of higher-density, affordable housing, the initiative models a new way to build consensus around community development goals. Supported by a team of design experts, facilitators, city planners, and development consultants, as well as market analysis resources and design tools, neighborhood partners and stakeholders create development guidelines to support housing that reflects neighborhood and city goals and respects the character of commercial corridors.

The initiative's overall goal is to create great neighborhoods that support housing choices for a mix of incomes and households, with access to transportation options, retail amenities, parks, and job opportunities. Whether redevelopment occurs in moderately large-scale projects or small infill sites, the goals are the same.

Phase 1 of the CHI attracted strong interest from neighborhood and resident organizations. Neighborhoods that wanted to participate had to go through a competitive proposal process, and competition in the final round of Phase 1 was quite intense. While it may seem unusual for neighborhoods to seek affordable and higher density housing, neighborhoods that wanted to participate in the initiative either desired more housing or could see development coming and wanted to influence how it would occur.

Each neighborhood project had a work group or steering committee that met regularly to determine project goals and outcomes, project work plan, and products. The group consisted of neighborhood and community representatives, the CHI coordinator, CHI partners, and appropriate members of the CHI technical team. The work groups met as often as needed, and some had subcommittees that worked on specific tasks. The CHI technical team consisted of people with expertise in the areas of City of Minneapolis policy, zoning and planning, and economic development; urban and architectural design; facilitation; citizen/community engagement; and community development.

Community groups that participated in the project were authorized by the city to coordinate citizen participation, and were administrators of the Neighborhood Revitalization Program for the City of Minneapolis (Martin and Pentel 2002). Phase 2 of the Corridor

---

The Corridor Housing Initiative in Brief

Purpose

The Corridor Housing Initiative is a proactive planning process intended to create viable development projects that include affordable housing options along transit corridors while meeting city goals and neighborhood interests.

People
- Community Partners
- Technical team (government, for-profit, and nonprofit entities)
    o   Coordinators: Center for Neighborhoods
    o   Facilitators: Center for Policy, Planning and Performance
    o   Design: Metropolitan Design Center
    o   Development: Central Community Housing Trust, Dewar Associates
    o   Government agencies

Common activities across most corridors
- Steering committee meetings with community partners and technical team over approximately six months
- "Block Workshop" exploring design and financing options for sites in the neighborhood, often held in conjunction with a public event such as a farmers market or festival
- Local property owner and business owner focus group
- Marketing meeting with developers
- Provision of resources about design and development issues, including housing density, types of housing, housing finance, and planning

Special activities as needed and within budgetary constraints
- Visual preference surveys conducted at an event such as a festival or in an active place such as a supermarket
- Workshops or questionnaires to identify community values
- Summaries of earlier planning work in the area
- Educational workshops for community members on building height and scale, pedestrian-oriented design, affordable housing, and livable neighborhoods
- Informational Web sites and online surveys of residents
- Neighborhood tours For residents

Final outputs
- Development guidelines or principles developed by steering committee to help developers understand local opportunities and values
- Neighborhoods better prepared to negotiate with developers

What it is not
- The Corridor Housing Initiative is not a master planning process, but its approach can be integrated with such processes

---

Housing Initiative extended to areas beyond Minneapolis, addressing cities that do not have organized neighborhood organizations. A new model is being developed that taps into other constituencies such as planning commissions and faith communities. The menu of activities and participants of a typical process is outlined in the sidebar.

For those involved in the process, there was a significant level of institutional learning. The five neighborhoods that participated in Phase I of the initiative were all very different in character, representing a range of socioeconomic circumstances (including ethnicity, incomes, and property values), technical and political capacities, and urban forms. Although the initiative envisioned similar approaches in each neighborhood, each evolved into a unique process that addressed the particular needs of the communities involved. In addition to the need to respond to local conditions as each community's process was implemented, the lessons learned by the technical team informed the development of subsequent processes.

While it is too early the gauge the program's success, in achieving a significant increase in affordable housing production, in 2005 CHI was a finalist for an Innovations in American Government award. The CHI approach seems so far to have a number of strengths related to the values and opportunities discussed earlier.

- *Scale*: In terms of physical scale, there are many levels at which a project can operate: global, regional, municipal, neighborhood, and site. The CHI focuses on sites at the neighborhood level, but places them in the context of municipal and regional policies and processes.
- *Mode of intervention*: There are many ways to increase housing: policies, funding, regulatory incentives, and specific site proposals but it is important to understand the strengths and weaknesses of different interventions, and the ones that are used in a specific situation need to be complementary. An initiative like CHI increases the political will to develop an integrated approach.
- *Constituencies*: The initiative has made infill development more appealing to key constituencies, such as governments, because it encourages broad participation and appeals to a variety of constituencies, including designers and developers who want to build and even advocates for preserving nature (compact development preserves natural areas on the urban edge). Focusing on development in transit corridors promotes mobility without automobile dependence and also may avoid NIMBYism if the area is understood to be earmarked for higher-density development.
- *Compatibility with several of the dominant urban visions*: While not all things to all people, the initiative's approach supports a number of value-based visions listed earlier: local democracy, personal mobility, individual housing choice, creating a sense of place, and compact, sustainable development with social inclusion.

Still, discussions among technical team members and a program evaluation by the Center for Policy, Planning and Performance (2005) show that the CHI faces challenges such as lack of site control, weak government support, limited funding, and managing neighborhood expectations.

Educational Objectives

So what kind of higher education can prepare people to break the pattern of urban development and reconstruct the city more creatively. How can people be prepared for dealing with the large-scale reconstruction of metropolitan areas by growing inward? How can a university-based program engage with the issues of scale, modes of intervention, constituencies, and vision highlighted in complex processes such as the Corridor Housing Initiative?

A solution involves several dimensions, including understanding the various values about urban life that need to be incorporated into a pattern of urban form that is to be widely adopted, dealing with the differences in scales of problems and responses, and developing institutional structures to support learning.

Values

For a development pattern to be produced at a large scale, it needs to fulfill a variety of values. Urban development can't be all things to all people, but in a market-based system it needs to sell to enough to be replicated (Forsyth 2005). In addition, local democracy means that development in existing areas must coincide with the values of the local electorate, at least to some extent. Resident acceptance, regulatory change, and development economics are key issues that often are dealt with in an abstract way, without the passion surrounding the visionary aspects.

Education can:
- Help identify values
- Provide a language for articulating values (Reich 1988)
- Provide tools for re-evaluating the built forms that flow from those values; for example, detached housing may not be the only way to satisfy a value of choice
- Emphasize the issue of large-scale replication
- Help future practitioners develop listening, analysis, and problem-solving skills

Scales of Vision

In the history of urban design, building in leftover spaces has not been a key approach. There are many good physical solutions to urban development problems on scales from the site to the region (Calthorpe and Fulton 2001; Congress for the New Urbanism 1998). However, even considering this, the ***grand vision*** for a big and bold solution has been favored. Grand visions can of course involve repairing and improving the city, but frequently they instead favor greenfield development or massive rebuilding. From the perspective of the industry, forms of ***mass production*** have been more crucial. Of course, the two are not mutually exclusive as it is possible to have a grand vision that involves mass production. In the design field, the ***unique increment***, a finely crafted building or garden, also is highly valued. Some are built in leftover spaces, but the most celebrated works are valued primarily for their uniqueness, giving them marginal value as an affordable housing solution.

A fourth kind of environmental intervention, the ***standardized increment***, is more useful for growing inward. This approach combines infill or building on leftover sites with some level of standardization for cost effectiveness. It works on fragmented sites in the context of different scales of concern. The challenge is to implement it in the United States, where governments are fragmented and weak and private interests dominate.

Education can:
- Identify or develop technologies and management systems for standardization on smaller sites
- Support the value of smaller-scale interventions in the city As alternatives to thegrand plans that tend to be valued in the development professions
- Give planning and policy students a deeper understanding of how interests, regulations, and economic processes work at different scales
- Prepare designers to put their work in political and economic context
- Train planners and designers to be conscious of different scales simultaneously

Institutional Structures
Universities are, of course, set up to deliver degree programs, but they can do much more. To better support inward urban development, universities can play three key roles: creating an urban center, convening urban experts, and providing non-degree urban education.

- Urban centers at universities take a number of forms, including the research center, university-based firm, community advocacy center, extension, studio, clearinghouse, umbrella/convening organization (Forsyth 2006). A number of these models, although not all, integrate students or recent graduates into research and outreach work and provide a mechanism for learning by doing.
- Universities, particularly those with a unique niche, can provide a neutral location for convening experts of various sorts to analyze the problems of urban areas and propose solutions. Students or faculty benefit by understanding the situation more comprehensively and, perhaps, being closer to power brokers.
- Urban problems are fast changing and shorter, non-degree educational programs can target emerging issues.

Educating urban professionals to help urban areas grow inward requires a flexible learning environment that mirrors the flexibility they will need in their future practice.

References

Burby, Raymond and Shirley Weiss. 1976. New communities USA. Lexington, MA: Lexington Books.

Calthorpe, Peter and William Fulton. 2001. The regional city: New urbanism and the end of sprawl. Washington, DC: Island Press.

Center for Neighborhoods. 2005. Corridor housing web pages. http://www.

center4neighborhoods.org/corridor_housing.htm.

Center for Policy, Planning, and Performance. 2005. Corridor Housing Initiative: Final Report. Draft. Prepared for the Center for Neighborhoods, February.

City of Minneapolis. 2005. Corridor housing web pages. http://www.ci.minneapolis. mn.us/cped/corridor_housing_strategy.asp.

Congress for the New Urbanism. 1998. Charter of the New Urbanism. http://www.cnu. org/cnu_reports/Charter.pdf.

Forsyth, Ann. 2005. Reforming suburbia: The planned communities of Irvine, Columbia, and The Woodlands. Berkeley: University of California Press.

Forsyth, Ann. 2005b. Urban Centers in Universities: Institutional Alternatives for Urban Design. *Journal of Urban Design* 11, 1: 97-103.

Hall, Peter. 1988. Cities of tomorrow. Oxford: Blackwell.

Martin, Judith A. and Paula Pentel. 2002. What the Neighbors Want: The Neighborhood Revitalization Program's First Decade., Journal of the American Planning Association 68, 4: 435-449. http://www.nrp.org/R2/News/IntheNews/APA20020920_1.html

Nelson, Arthur C. 2004. Toward a new metropolis: The opportunity to rebuild America. A discussion paper prepared for the Brookings Institution Metropolitan Policy Program.

Reich, Robert. 1988. Policy making in a democracy. In The power of public ideas. Robert Reich ed. Cambridge, Massachusetts: Ballinger.

Ward, Stephen. 2002. Planning the twentieth-century city. Chichester: Wiley.

Yabes, Ruth. 2005. Draft book manuscript on collaborative learning.

Chapter 6
Environmental Expertise And Civic Ecology: Linking the University and its Metropolitan Community

Frank Fischer

Introduction

Efforts to develop environmental expertise have largely emphasized the technical aspects of sustainable urban development over basic normative issues inherent to both its definition and realization, including the role of citizen participation. Insofar as most of our environmental problems have local roots, the role of citizen engagement takes on special importance, a point underscored by Agenda 21 of the Rio Earth Summit and its provisions in Local Agenda 21 (United Nations 1992) – both of which spell out the basic contours of sustainability.

Among the forces in the path of such citizen involvement has been the kind of professional education offered by the urban university and its environmental programs, in particular the environmental planning and policy sciences, disciplines that still rest in significant part on outmoded "neopositivist" epistemological assumptions and the technocratic practices derived from them. For this reason, this chapter calls for a broader public or "civic-ecological" reorientation that methodologically integrates the technical and the normative aspects of environmental problems, particularly one that facilitates more cooperative, interactive knowledge relationships between experts and the public.

Such a reorientation is important not only for the revitalizing of citizen participation – the cornerstone of a democratic government – but also for improving both the legitimacy and effectiveness of environmental policy development and implementation. Toward this end, the chapter offers suggestions as to how environmental education might be redesigned, and proposes practical activities to promote metropolitan civic ecology through cooperative activities on the part of faculty, graduate students, and engaged citizens.

Insofar as the knowledge and authority of expertise hinders the citizen's role in a policy field laden with complex technical considerations, the question becomes all the more pressing. Since environmentalism first emerged, ecological protection became increasingly a matter given over to technical and scientific expertise. Indeed, environmental policy deliberations now are generally carried out in a technical language that more or less excludes the citizen's voice. In response, environmental activists have themselves been compelled to professionalize. Ecologists, natural resource economists, and environmental lawyers have assumed leadership positions within the leading environmental organizations, also at the expense of citizen participation.

As the professionalization of environmentalism gave rise to a rapid expansion of university curricula – from ecology and environmental medicine to environmental law and planning – environmental decision making became embedded in the technical languages of cost-benefit analysis, technology assessment, and risk-benefit analysis. This "technocratization" of environmental policy has largely relegated citizens to the status of audience, as industry-affiliated experts and environmental counter-experts publicly debated the merits of their competing assessments.

Although the movement was the product of citizen activism, often in the face of scientific opposition, this professionalization has neglected the important inputs – both normative and empirical – that citizens can bring to the deliberative process. On the normative side, they bring social values and legitimacy to the process. On the empirical side, they can supply "local knowledge" not readily accessible to the experts, but essential for effective policy making.

In more recent years, as part of the turn to "sustainability," we have come to recognize the need to find ways to build citizens back into the process, but it has not proven easy. One major problem has been – and continues to be – the nature of expert practices, built on epistemological traditions that have long sought to replace the citizen's normative reason with scientifically "value-neutral" knowledge. While the problem now receives partial acknowledgement, at least in some circles, little has been done to ameliorate it. Indeed, in many of the most influential academic institutions, the technocratic understanding of the environment is very much alive and well. For this reason, we turn next to a more specific examination of the nature of professional knowledge as it pertains to the environmental problem and the technical practices derived from it. Toward this end, the focus is on environmental planning and policy analysis.

Professional Expertise and the Environmental Crisis

The professions of planning and the policy sciences have largely developed a technical understanding of the environmental crisis. These disciplines are basically the product of an epistemology called positivism. The technical rationalism of this mode of thought differentiates a technocratic consciousness from other worldviews and cultural orientations. This rationalistic worldview has been a fairly ambiguous, if not arrogant, epistemological assumption – namely that the positivist method is the only valid means of obtaining "true knowledge." Only such knowledge is still today seen to supply the basis for solutions to many of our economic and social problems; it is also said to facilitate the rational design of social systems in ways that enable us to better produce and manage, if not altogether eliminate, the persistent conflicts and crises that now plague modern society.

More concretely, neopositivism gives shape to an abstract, technical formulation of society and its problems. Social problems, conceptualized in technical terms, are freed from the cultural, psychological, and linguistic contexts that constitute the lens of social tradition. Breaking the recipes of "tradition" and "ordinary knowledge" through the power of its unique abstract language, the neopositivist form of thought creates an illusion of cultural and historical transcendence, which, in turn, sustains a sense of political, cultural, and moral neutrality. In pursuit of the most efficient problem-solving strategies, typically expressed in the precise but abstract models of mathematics, experts appear to objectively transcend partisan interests. Their technical methodologies and modes of decision making are said to strive for value neutrality, if they are not in fact "value free."

This technical   "value-neutral" – understanding of social action is manifested through an administrative conceptualization of problem solving and policy formation. Basic to managerial strategy, the objective is to move as many political and social decisions as possible into the realm of administrative decision making, where they can be defined and accessed in technical terms. Vexing economic and social problems thus are interpreted as issues in need of improved administrative design and technical decision-making; their solutions are to be found through the application of managerial techniques, including the planning and policy sciences. It is a conviction fundamental to contemporary technocratic strategy.

Inherent to this strategy is a subtle, and sometimes not so subtle, form of authoritarianism. Once the idea that we can empirically calculate and administratively design "the right way" to accomplish our goals is accepted, there is little reason to engage in the exploration of other views. The "rational" person is the one who agrees to submit to the properly derived technical and administrative knowledge of the experts. The authority of the expert, from this perspective, should take precedence over the democratic exchange of opinions.

Underlying the hubris of this position rests an anthropocentric view of the world. With no small arrogance, "technocratic man" has managed to construe humankind's unique powers of the mind as legitimations for his own rapacious appropriation of the physical world. Nature, in short, is tamed and subordinated to serve man's own economic needs. Emphasizing what is seen as the mechanistic character of the physical laws governing nature, the technocratic worldview takes nature's creator – much like the technocrat himself – to be something of an engineer. Organized according to the laws of nature – human as well as physical – the everyday world thus can be conceptualized as a configuration of "problems" to be technically and administratively engineered by experts.

The repercussions of this worldview today are readily apparent. The most striking example is the ecological crisis. What began several hundred years ago as the techno-industrial exploitation of nature's resources for unlimited industrial progress today constitutes a serious ecological problem. Although substantial amounts of research and development monies are being poured into the search for solutions, much of this effort appears to miss the point. By and large, it is governed by the same kind of technocratic thinking that gave rise to the problem in the first place. Rather than looking for new relationships between technology and nature (emphasizing conservation and a more efficient planning and control of economic growth), experts plunge forward on the premise that future technological and administrative advances will get us out of our present fix. Ignoring the need for a new "existential balance" among the factor of production – technology, nature, and human purpose, in particular – the technocratic response to the ecological crisis is proving to be the paradigmatic example of metaphysical crisis.

Technocratic consciousness can be understood as a failure to identify and maintain a clear distinction between two basic modes of reason, one technical and the other normative. Each of these forms of reason pertains to different and autonomous realms of human activity. Whereas the sphere of economic production is governed by technical criteria, the world of everyday social life (including family, culture, religion, and politics) is negotiated through normative reason. Although in reality each sphere is deeply intertwined with the other, analytically they must be conceptualized as separate spheres governed by different modes of reason. Technocratic consciousness thus fails to recognize the boundaries appropriate to the application of technical criteria to the society as whole. Through its unquestioned belief in technological and material progress, technocratic intelligence obscures an underlying epistemological concatenation of the two separate realms of human activity. Planners and managers blur the lines between the worlds of economic production and social interaction, thus making it difficult for many to distinguish between the priorities of the economic system and those of their own lives. It is not that people should reject economic and technological progress, but rather that they should establish their own relationships to it through processes of intersubjective discourse. This failure to examine the fundamental value questions raised by economic and technological progress present a deep seated paradox: As technologically based affluence increases in advanced industrial societies, so does the sense of goal-lessness, drift, and insecurity among the citizens who benefit from it.

Sustainable Development as Normative Construct

It is not that technical considerations are irrelevant to the question, but rather the need is to look as well into the ways that ecological degradation is more fundamentally a sociocultural problem related to our way of life. Toward this end, we need to better understand how the technical dimensions of ecology are interwoven with complex social, intellectual, and institutional realities that create the environmental problem. Rather than permit the utilitarian criteria of environmental economists and planners to neglect basic questions concerning the nature of social needs and the extant patterns of consumption, as well as the art of reflecting on them, we need to engage in genuine discussion about needs and values. Instead of substituting for such discussion with techniques such as risk and liability assessment, we need to first engage in normative discussion about the more basic sociocultural aspects of sustainability. The task thus is to find a sustainable balance between the technical and the social.

The challenge is readily apparent in the struggle to define and shape the concept of sustainability. Sustainable development, as initially advanced, is an inherently normative concept aimed at redressing the ecological imbalances among industrial development, environmental degradation, human health, and the social relations underlying them. Through the concept of intergenerational equity, sustainable development depends on answers to a host of profoundly important questions – normative questions – about the responsibility of present societies and their communities to the future; the relation of the rich to the poor; the distribution of the costs involved in environmental clean-up; questions about the relative merits of relying on markets or states; the relationship of individual freedoms to the collective good; and our appropriate relationship to other species.

Since the concept of sustainability was first popularized, however, environmental planners and policy agencies have steadily mis-translated the concept into a technical strategy for programmatic reform of existing socioeconomic relationships. It is an approach often called "ecological modernization" (emphasizing technology, cost-benefit analysis, and market strategies), a strategy designed to technically guide the management future of advanced industrial society. Toward this end, universities now train sustainable development experts to think in terms of calculating and planning the "carrying capacities" of regional and local ecosystems through the efficient application of such "ecoknowledge."

In the textbook, all of this might sound good. But in the real world of environmental politics, the assumptions upon which the strategy is built are estimable. Most obvious is the fact that our knowledge is nowhere sophisticated enough to reveal the limits of nature, thus permitting us to exploit resources safely up to that limit. We are, for example, only barely beginning to develop the capability to measure the phenomenon of climate change. The idea that we might literally monitor and manage such environmental change with the kinds of precision suggested by these sustainable development experts is more a scientific ideology than a certainty within our reach, especially not within the critical timeframe necessitated by global warming.

Because science cannot answer with any certainty the critical questions about both the nature and implications of such complex environmental issues, they remain open to interpretation. In such situations, technical interpretation is easily translated into political disagreement. Each party to the dispute can use interpretative ambiguity to argue the case according to their own needs and interests. Those who support action to stem the growth of greenhouse gases can point to the amassing evidence. Those who oppose the costs of such interventions can stress that it has in no final way been proven. In such cases, science actually intensifies rather than mitigates environmental politics. Instead of solving the problem, science only becomes another sort of political ammunition that interest groups and their counter-experts fire at one another (Fischer 1990).

Beyond this inability to provide widely accepted scientific predictions, the technocratic approach poses a subtler, but much more politically significant concern related to the very definition of environmental problems. In order to technically frame an environmental problem, it is necessary to hold constant the basic structures and processes of society. This is typically achieved by assuming people's common interests in dealing with environmental efforts. While this might seem to encourage unified environmental action, it tends to conceal the economic assumptions, social choices, and risks that in fact block such action. By holding existing social and political structures constant, such models serve to draw attention away from the competing interests of different social groups and nations that are basic to understanding the causes of the problem, let alone the complicated political task of shaping acceptable solutions. Most basic are the conflicting interests among the rich developed and the poor developing regions of the world. Such inattention to national and localized political economies almost ensures that scientists, both natural and social, will continue to be surprised by emerging conflicts and the failed predictions to which they contribute. By setting the problem outside the context of social conflict, the "neutral and objective" pretences of scientific and technological solutions further work to block effective political consensus building.

Once the problem is analytically abstracted from the political realm, citizens and their governments tend to be separated from the environmental consequences of their actions; it obscures their need to assume responsibility for the outcomes. By treating environmental degradation as the negative *effect* of the social and economic activities that characterize our daily lives instead of everyday life as the *cause* of the degradation, scientists can concentrate on finding "technical fixes" to mitigate problematic side effects. Such solutions, of course, merely focus on pollution at the "end-of-the pipe" rather than on the more challenging task of reinventing production processes to eliminate the need for the pipe. As such, they cover over the need to examine how pollution is more fundamentally a sociocultural problem related to our way of life.

Many fear an effort to open the door to a broader political examination of the underlying assumptions of the environmental problem. Indeed, this is one of the key concerns that attracts people to the technocratic approach. For them, the technical problem is weighty enough; attaching it to a whole host of conflictual questions about our competing ways of life – issues about the social distribution of wealth, political participation, corporate control, government regulation, etc. – is only to court political gridlock (Bast et al. 1994). Without necessarily denying the pressing nature of these social and economic problems, the urgency of the environmental problem should exempt it from such considerations. This argument, in fact, has led some to argue for a kind of environmental technocracy (Ophuls 1977). In this view, we are best advised to turn over these questions to an enlightened environmental elite capable of making the tough decisions based on the technical facts of the situation (Bahro 1987).

The argument, however, fails to confront the socio-technical foundation of the environmental problem – which is another way to say there is no escape from dealing with the underlying assumptions; environmental politics ultimately turns on them. In this regard, there is a twofold challenge.

First is the scientific task of building analytical models capable of including in the dynamic effects social as well as natural systems and how each influences the other. Basic here is to learn how to link models of endangered ecosystems with the human actions and sociopolitical processes that foster and sustain them. It is especially important to discover how to interconnect the local and global levels. Such research involves figuring out how to account for the fact that regions have a certain autonomy in terms of global dynamics, as well as the fact that bioregions and social systems often do not coincide in space and time.

Even more important for present purposes is the second challenge concerning the policy implications drawn from such models. That is, how do we move from an analytical understanding of the environment to the political task of forging a policy consensus around a particular model of the problem? Insofar as each conceptual model of the environmental problem portends a particular impact on the sociopolitical world, the affected groups invariably seek to represent their own interests. Because the policy concerns raise complicated issues of burden-sharing, especially between the rich and the poor, it is inevitable that each negatively affected group will do more than merely examine the technical data. Straight away, they zero in on the assumptions that differentiate their ways of life. If the assumptions are disputed, the analysis is little more than a useless exercise.

The question, then, is how do we take action in face of both scientific uncertainties and relative socioeconomic inequalities? The answer is found in political coalition building. Beyond technical analysis, environmental solutions have little value unless they can generate the political consensus necessary to adopt and implement them. For this reason, there is no choice but to open the environmental debate to a wider discussion of the economic and social assumptions upon which it rests. Viewed in this way, we have to turn the problem upside down. Before technical analysis can play a meaningful role, we need to come to basic understandings about who gets what, when, and how. Toward this end, citizens and the larger public need to be brought into the policy deliberations.

Given the nature of the social and political conflicts that accompany environmental deliberation, this is, of course, a formidable assignment. It means the development of a more participatory form of democratic decision making than generally practiced in contemporary Western societies. It requires creating innovative new mechanisms for bringing together scientific expertise and democratic political deliberation.

The foregoing discussion makes clear that much of environmental problem lies beyond the reach of the environmental professions as they have been structured. Environmental problems, as we have seen, are as much political and social problems as they are scientific. Finding answers to those questions depends on developing more sophisticated analytical apparatus or scientific theories and also on refining the processes by which communities can debate their differences and arrive (if possible) at a consensus. Determining how the environment and preferred environmental futures can be defined and measured scientifically – whether in terms of sustainability, or climatic stability, or ecosystem integrity, for example – must be informed by, and contribute to, these political processes. What has been missing up to this point is an integrated approach that is both scientific and normative.

A number of basic normative issues point to the need for such a reorientation. One has to do with the normative dimensions inherent to our understanding and construction of environmental issues themselves. A second has to do with the relation of norms and values to our traditional conception of science itself. Third, there is the need for an interpretive orientation resulting from the high levels of uncertainty associated with many aspects of the range of environmental problems. Finally, a more collaborative relationship with lay citizens is needed to implement policy proposals. Together, these gaps make clear the need for a multiperspective, interdisciplinary, interpretive framework for professional education and practices.

To say that the problem is both scientific and normative involves much more than bringing in political philosophers to have parallel discussions. In the broader context, it is necessary to rethink the relationship of science to political and social philosophy. We need to better understand the interrelationships between them, where they come together and where they don't. Short of that, we will continue to reproduce the unproductive interactions that have – and continue – to take place. In the current situation, both empirically and normatively oriented experts vaguely acknowledge one another, but mainly go on doing what they have traditionally done. Required instead is a new epistemological understanding of these interactions. As I have argued elsewhere, this involves replacing the scientific framework with a multi-dimensional postempiricist perspective that recognizes the place of both empirical and normative modes of reason (Fischer 1995, 2003). This shift rests on an epistemological justification draw from contemporary work in science studies and social constructivism.

Rethinking Expertise: Social Constructivism and Post-Empiricism

From the social constructivist analysis of scientific activity, we learn that the endeavor is already filled with interpretive elements. Although scientists describe their activities in terms of objective data, this work shows that what we call a fact often is built on subjective social assumptions. Interpretive judgments have to be made throughout the scientific process, and some are matters for which the scientific community has no privileged status. While few, if any, of these judgments make it into the final scientific report, they often play a definitive role in what comes to be the consensus that emerges. In this regard, what is called science at any particular time is as much an informed consensus as it is a set of hard facts. This means that there are various openings in which others concerned with normative questions have legitimate issues, although they seldom are asked to contribute to the deliberation forming the consensus.

None of this means that science, whether physical or social, should not be taken seriously. It means rather that what we call "science" has to be understood as a more subtle interaction between physical and social factors. Whatever constitutes scientific knowledge at any particular time has to be seen as more than the product of empirically confirmed experiments and tests. Such knowledge claims are better described as scientific *interpretations* or *beliefs* based on an amalgam of technical and normative judgments. In some cases, the technical judgments are more decisive than in others, but both technical and social considerations are always involved (with the mix between the two remaining a question to be empirically examined case by case). Influenced by many more factors than "the pursuit of truth," such claims have to be understood as the relative product of a community of practitioners who establish the evidential criteria and guide the research processes through which truth claims are decided. The communities that render these opinions, as historical and sociological analysis show, constitute hierarchies of practitioners organized in significant part around their own internal power structures, interests, and status claims (Kuhn 1970).

Such studies also help us recognize that scientific communities are not the only bodies capable of making judgments about the same reality. From competing perspectives, other groups grounded in different forms of rationality can make relevant judgments about the same phenomena. Historically, the determination of whose rationality prevails has largely been decided by those wielding the most influence or power. Invariably these determinations are subject to future challenges and new technical findings have always played an important role in such confrontations. But their role has generally been mediated by changing beliefs. Contrary to the official line, new findings alone have seldom been decisive. The advance of knowledge, in short, cannot be understood as a linear process driven by research methodologies.

In this understanding, facts, in the natural as well as the social world, depend upon underlying assumptions and meanings. What is taken to be a fact is in effect the decision of a particular community of inquirers who work within the set of theoretical presuppositions to which they subscribe. Customarily, of course, we simply accept a particular view of the world; the presuppositions that undergird it seldom come into question. This makes it possible, at least most of the time, to treat large parts of the world as natural and given. While such an organization of reality facilitates communication and understanding between social actors, it cannot in and of itself serve as an adequate basis for social research. Beyond seeking to explain a "given" reality, social science must also attempt to explain how social groups construct their own understandings of that reality. Not only do such constructions constitute the most basic level of social meanings relevant to the world of social action, their implications are fundamental to an understanding of the processes of social change, without which we would have little need for social science.

Seen in this light, neopositivism's attempt to fix a given set of social and political arrangements tends to reify a particular reality. From the constructivist perspective, we see that the outcomes of such research can at best be relevant only to the particular socio-historical understandings of reality from which they are abstracted. In so far as empiricist social science's emphasis on "objective reality" diverts attention from the struggles grounded in "other realities" that challenge existing arrangements, social science – wittingly or unwittingly – serves as much to provide ideological support for a configuration of power as it does to explain it.

The more applied the science, the more important it is to recognize this role involved in the inquiry process. First, the world of applied science – applied social science in particular – is always designed to inform the world of action. This world also is a construction fusing empirical and normative considerations. Of particular importance is the matter of social relevance. The actors in a particular situation will have particular motives and goals that will render some empirical findings relevant to their context and other not so relevant. Given that an implied science, like environmental planning, is always designed to serve such deliberations, the decision process always has to bring technical and normative considerations together in an interpretive arrangement. Even when environmental regulatory rules are established as general rules, they nonetheless are applied to specific contexts. To be effectively applied, their application has to be negotiated with the normative and empirical facts of the situation – e.g., in matters related to biodiversity, some areas have wildlife zones while others do not.

A second consideration that necessitates an interpretive perspective is uncertainty. In the matter of risk, for example, the degree to which science can answer and resolve the question is limited, often quite limited. For this reason, the decision-making process always has to weigh considerations against each other. What is the best thing to do under the circumstances? Should we return to nuclear power because of global warming? Should people move away from the nuclear power plant? And so on.

Another way to describe this post-empiricist interpretive framework is in terms of a multi-disciplinary perspective. Decisions under such circumstances are best reached by looking at things from different perspectives, both scientific and normative. With regard to science, we speak continually about interdisciplinary research, but we don't know that much about how to do it, thanks to the established boundaries that continue because of the institutional rewards associated with them. Thus, while we put scientific ecologists and environmental social scientists in the same group, they mainly do their own thing, often criticizing the others afterwards. Also, little noticed in this respect is that science itself is not all of a piece. The physicist employs a different mode of reason and explanation than the biologist, although we think of both of them as doing science.

To this mix we need to add the range of competing normative perspectives that can judge the value implications of the different choices and assess them against the goals of the communities at issue. At specific points, this also includes lay people. Not only do they often possess particular facts of the situation that are needed by the decision makers, their legitimation and motivation frequently are essential for the commitment necessary for effective implementation of environmental regulations. This fact has led others to focus on participatory or collaborative research, or what we shall call here civic ecology, a topic to which we return in the second half of the chapter.

The integration of empirical and normative inquiry requires a framework of practical reason that organizes and guides such deliberation. Such a framework includes technical information but situates it within the situational, societal, and ideological contexts in which public policies are embedded (Fischer 1995). It is an approach that can go a considerable distance toward overcoming the resistance of citizens to scientific analysis. To this end, the task is to set up a dialectical relationship between the theoretical knowledge of the expert and the socio-cultural information of the citizens.

From this perspective, planners and policy analysts need practical training in the art of analytic and normative interpretation. Included in the exercise would be the role of the citizen and lay knowledge in the deliberative process. Here one would address questions such as when would the citizen have something of particular importance to offer, and when would the assessment best remain a matter of interdisciplinary professional judgment?

In the process, the environmental policy professional has to learn to appreciate that environmental policy, as an applied research methodology, is always addressed to the world of action and, as such, is necessarily situated inside a practical/normative discourse. Rather than understanding normative discourse as an inferior form of reason relied on in the face of empirical uncertainty or a general inability to deal intellectually with the rigors of technical analysis, the planning and policy sciences community has to come to grips with the fact their research questions not only emerge from the world of action, but that the acceptability of their findings also must be judged ultimately by normative standards. That is, epistemologically speaking, their scientific findings of necessity have to be judged within the societal context to which they apply. Social context, both local and societal, has to be understood as part of the knowledge essential to the evaluation. This involves a different kind of logic and deliberation. Scientists fail to see this because of their irrational attachment to one component of a larger assessment (Fischer 2003). They have a contribution to make, but so do others adhering to other modes of reason, including citizens. Indeed, this becomes the theoretical basis for civic ecology.

Civic Ecology: Citizens and Experts in Collaborative Inquiry

Civic environmentalism or ecology is more than an academic idea put together for conferences. It is an emerging activity with thousands of projects around the world that bring public-oriented professionals together with citizens to confront local and regional environmental problems (DeWitt 1994; Rubin 2002; Shutkin 2000). Civic ecology, as it is developing, is a distinctive approach to environmental science and policy that encourages citizen participation and deliberative decision making by civic stakeholders (Sirianni and Friedland 2001). It draws on the theory and practice of a variety of interrelated community-based endeavors, such as civic environmentalism, conservation and sustainable development, collaborative natural resource management, participatory action research, and related innovations in participatory environmental governance and transboundary ecosystem management. It seeks to create common ground for envisioning desired future conditions for sustainable ecosystems and the possibility of implementing such a vision through the facilitation of citizen-based public discourse.

As a practice, civic ecology exists at the intersection of three important currents in the contemporary environmental arena. The first is the need for collaborative dialogue across the many ecological, sociological, cultural, and political-institutional processes that divide environmentally concerned scientists, policy makers, activists, and citizens. The second is the growing recognition of the need for community members to gather their local knowledge and bring it to bear on the search for solutions to problems – both local and global – that effect their communities. Third is the importance of developing a common understanding and vision of a sustainable relationship of humankind to nature at all levels of settlement, from local and regional to global. Inherent to all three of these currents of civic ecology is a cooperative relationship between experts and citizens. Although we have come to recognize the importance of this relationship, we are only beginning to examine and better understand the dynamics between these two different cognitive orientations.

From this perspective, an important piece of professional reform involves rethinking and restructuring the citizen-expert relationship. Given that the expert needs the citizens' perspectives, the expert has to enter into an interactive relationship with the policy-relevant citizens. This means retreating from the traditions of a hierarchical top-down relationship supported by the ideology of technical rationality and developing new models of collaborative or participatory inquiry. In the first instance, this can be seen as an issue of democracy (Martell 1994; Morrision 1995). But it is now also recognized as a requirement for problem-solving. Citizens, in short, have a type of information not available to the experts – or at least they have no privileged position in this matter. The expert can at best function here as a "citizen expert" (Fischer 2000).

Expertise, toward this end, has to take on the additional function of facilitating deliberation. Although this conception of the expert's role differs sharply from the standard understanding, it is not as new to the policy literature as it might seem. Already in the 1920s Dewey (1927) argued that the future of a meaningful democracy would depend on the possibility of finding new forms of collaboration between experts and citizens. Following Dewey's lead, Harold Lasswell (1951), the founder of the policy science movement, envisioned the role of the social scientific policy professional as that of a "clarifer" of issues for public deliberation. Like Dewey, he called for an improvement of methods and conditions of debate, discussion, and persuasion. Public debate would require the participation of experts, but rather than merely analyze and render judgments per se, they would interpret and present complex issues in ways that facilitate citizen learning and empowerment. Unfortunately, the scientific community has understood this challenge only in technical terms, namely to supply the techno-empirical information to supply the debate. In the process, they have advanced the technocratic assumption that such information plays the essential role in such deliberations.

The following discussion sketches out a number of institutional activities that emerge from and support the effort to better understand and develop these cooperative relationships. They are designed to serve two interrelated purposes. On the one hand, they involve a set of activities designed to help develop the concept and practice of civic ecology. While the epistemological and political arguments underlying the need for these practices are available, the actual experiences needed to work them out are either missing or underdeveloped. Thus, the university can profitably engage in a series of university-community interactions aimed at exploring cooperative inquiry, both experimentally and practically. These endeavors can be the source of experiences and discussion about how to reform the curriculum, and at the same time offer the community the kind of experiences that make civic ecology meaningful.

Toward this end, four different sets of interrelated activities associated with an interdisciplinary faculty of environmental studies are presented: public environmental education, environmental science shops, participatory environmental inquiry, and environmentally oriented citizens' juries. The university, it is argued, should be the site for such activities; its faculty and students should develop efforts to help facilitate these practices with local community members. The next section outlines each activity and suggests how the university can faciliate these them.

Linking the Public University and its Civic Environment

Linking the university and its surrounding community is – or at least was – a venerable model of the public university. The original mission of the public land grant college was to work closely with communities to help them meet both their educational and research needs. While the model focused primarily on agricultural communities, the concept applies equally to the ecological community, especially as it relates to assisting in the development of civic ecology. Not only would such an orientation help citizens initiate studies related to the pressing environmental problems confronting their metropolitan areas, it would also assist them in understanding how to carry out the research and in deciding how to assess and use its results. At the same time, such a relationship would help the university gain more support from its taxpaying neighbors, as well as assist the faculty in developing more relevant local curriculua. Beyond the faculty, such community-based research activities can involve graduate and undergraduate students. It can, in this way, unite all of the basic university missions – research, teaching, and service – in creative ways that enliven each other (Cordes 1998). In the process, it can give added practical meaning to the learning that takes place in an educational curriculum.

Public Environmental Education
The most obvious activity that connects the university to its community is education (Bowers 1995; Orr 1992). But most university education either is not readily available to many members of the local community or is not relevant to their needs and interests. For this reason, the university-community link requires a different set of commitments.

It is not that the standard forms of education need to be replaced, but rather they need to be integrated with different forms of knowledge relevant to sustainable development. Already we have seen that the reform of professional practices needs the benefit of such interactions. Thus, while courses and lectures typically are directed to other scientists and would-be scientists, generally centering on the latest research topics or findings, public presentations should be focused on the practical aspects of environmental issues relevant to citizens' everyday lives. In addition to helping stimulate environmental awareness, and more specifically interest in civic ecology, these lectures are a public contribution to the local citizens themselves. Public universities frequently speak about the need to develop better community relations, and this would be one way to do that. It also would provide a platform for the issues to be discussed in the activities described below, environmental science shops, community-based environmental research, and citizens' juries.

The proposed adult-oriented courses should cover topics ranging from very practical everyday environmental issues, such as garbage collection, transportation, energy conservation, and air pollution to courses about the larger issues to which they are connected – for example, global warming and its relation to air pollution, energy, and transportation, related to larger issues such as ozone and its consequences. Basic to these courses should be the nature of local action and its necessity for effective environmental amelioration, including local-global lineages. Toward this end, the participants should learn of practical examples from other parts of the country and the world more generally, emphasizing both their successes and failures. And not least important, they should be taught in the ordinary language of the citizen. Citizens should learn how to understand technical issues, but not in ways that intimidate or mystify. To some degree, the model already exists. It is the approach that many physics departments have adopted for university students required to take science courses as elective requirements, often described as "Physics for Poets."

Environmental Science Shops
One proposed activity to make good on the commitment to the community and the region would be built on the model of the "science shop" developed in the Netherlands (Sclove 1995). In the 1970s, Dutch universities established a network of public-oriented science shops to respond to the concerns of community groups, public interest organizations, and trade unions about social, environmental, and technological issues. Each shop employed staff and student interns to screen questions and refer challenging problems to university volunteers. During the shop's formative years, faculty members generally performed the research, although later graduate and undergraduate students did much of the work under faculty supervision. Students who participate often receive university credit, and sometimes turn their investigations into graduate theses or adapt their career plans as a result of the experiences. Because students are doing research and writing papers, and faculty members are supervising and evaluating their work, both groups are doing what they would be doing as part of their regular workload; thus the extra cost and time are minimal.

Community questions are accepted if the inquiring group lacks the resources to pay for research, is not commercially motivated, and would be able to use the research results as a basis for action. Some science shops also accept socially oriented inquiries from organizations – such as national environmental groups or local governments – that can contribute to the cost of the undertaking research. The science shop approach has helped workers evaluate environmental and technology issues and has addressed issues such as the employment consequences of new production processes, the life circumstances of disaffected teenagers, and the market potential for an independent women's radio station.

Science shops have spread throughout Europe and are receiving support from the European Union (Jorgensen, Hall, and Hall 2004). The United States has no comparable network to the Dutch system. In the late 1970s, the U.S. National Science Foundation offered to support similar activities through its Science for Citizens Program. But the program was terminated abruptly in the Reagan years. Nonetheless, across the country there have been a variety of projects that approximate science shops. The time is ripe for a renewal of this initiative.

Community-Based Environmental Research
The second activity, which can be closely likened to the science shop, is community-based participatory research (Fischer 2000; Hills and Mullett 2000). In this approach, community members conduct their own research with the assistance of a professional. The expert facilitates the research project, helping citizens decide how to design the research process, collect the data, and interpret it. Of the numerous examples of such activities, most have been associated with research related to the community itself. Many have involved questions related to toxic waste problems.

Community-based participatory research is a form of inquiry that is conducted by members of the community (e.g., with civic, grassroots, or worker groups through civil society). It includes, for example, action research and participatory research (Heron 1996). "Community" is defined as a geographic region, but includes communities of interest, occupation, history, or language. Among the more prominent examples, such participatory research involves the collaboration of community workers (represented by grassroots activists, community-based organizations, workers) and experts (represented by university researchers, professional scientists, etc.). At its best, the outcome of such collaboration is seen to have significant, long-lasting results that reflect the investment of each party and the benefits of working together.

Frequently, this movement has drawn on the experiences of "participatory research" based on the work of the late Brazilian educator, Paolo Freire (1973). In this model, an expert helps the community plan and organize the task. It is, as such, a task of facilitation. Basic to this work is the theory and facilitation of adult learning. Participant learning is defined as enlarging the citizens'/clients' abilities to pose the problems and questions that interest and concern them and helping connect them to information and resources to help them (Brookfield 1986). As a technique of empowerment and self-help, facilitation is defined as challenging learners with different ways of examining and interpreting their experience and presenting them with ideas and behaviors that assist them in critically exploring political issues in terms of their own ways of acting, their value systems, and the assumptions by which they live.

Citizens' Juries in Environmental Policy Making

One of the most important innovations designed to bring citizens and experts together during recent decades has been "consensus conferences" or "citizen juries" first developed by the Danish Board of Technology. Consensus conferences were developed to find new and innovative ways to get around the divisive conflicts associated with environmentally risky technologies. They are designed to integrate expertise with a wide range of social, economic, and political perspectives (Joss and Durant 1995). In Denmark, these "citizen's tribunals" have taken place in the Danish Parliament, dealing with issues that stood before it. These conferences are widely recognized to have bridged the gap between scientific experts, politicians, and the citizenry.

The formal goals of the consensus conference are twofold: to provide members of parliament and other decision makers with relevant information and to stimulate public discussion through media coverage of both the conference and the follow-up debates. Typically, conducting such a conference involves bringing together 10 to 25 citizens charged with the task of assessing a socially sensitive topic of science and technology. The lay participants usually are selected from written replies to advertisements announced in national newspapers and radio broadcasts. A facilitator work is closely with the panel, guiding the participants through an organized set of rules and procedures. In addition to organizing the preparatory informational and deliberative processes, the facilitator chairs the conference. Somewhat like a judge in a jury trial, the facilitator's task is to maintain the experts' focus on the lay panel's questions during the conference and assist panelists in finding the most direct answers to their questions.

Not only do the citizens frame their own questions, they can pursue the kinds of information they find necessary to answer them. Panelists are supplied with extensive reading materials by the steering committee and given a substantial interval of time to study the materials at home. The steering committee uses the participants' lists of questions to assemble additional information for the panelists and to identify an interdisciplinary group of technological and environmental experts to make presentations to the citizen panel. In some cases, a hearing is also organized for parties interested in the selected subject. Such groups – e.g., individuals or companies with extensive knowledge, influence, and/or dependence on the field; research institutions; research committees; traditional interest groups; and grassroots organizations – are given an opportunity to contribute information to the deliberative process.

At the end of the process, usually on the third day of the meeting, the citizen panel retires to deliberate on the exchanges. With the assistance of a secretary supplied by the steering committee, the group prepares a consensus report (averaging 15 to 30 pages long). Typically, the report reflects the range of interests and concerns of parties involved in the conference. Beyond scientific and technical considerations, it speaks to the spectrum of economic, legal, ethical, and social aspects associated with the topic. Upon completion of the report, the citizen panel publicly presents its conclusions, often in a highly visible setting in the presence of the media, a variety of experts, and the general public. Subsequently, the report is distributed to politicians, scientists, special interest groups, and the public.

In the United States, a pilot project dealing with the topic of telecommunications was conducted in Boston in 1997 by the Loka Institute. Also, the University of North Carolina experimented with a computer-based consensus conference on genetic engineering. These experiences have shown that a consensus conference is an excellent way to both invigorate contemporary democratic practices and build understanding and trust among citizens and experts. The approach is a first-rate source of information and experience for better understanding the relationships upon which civic ecology would be built.

Conclusion

The discussion has outlined the limits of the technical conception of the planning and policy sciences, environmental planning and policy in particular, and illustrated them in terms of the normative requirements of sustainable development. The normative dimensions of sustainable development, as spelled out by the Brundtland Commission (1987) and other scholarly works, require social equity through political consensus shaped by active public participation, or what here has been called civic ecology. In this view, the planning and policy professions are in need of an alternative methodological perspective; the suggested solution is to move beyond the neopositivist foundations that have shaped these disciplines to a post empiricist approach based on social constructivism and practical reason, an approach capable of integrating both the empirical and normative dimensions of sustainable development on their own terms.

Toward this end, the discussion turned to ways this framework could be employed to redesign the practices of the policy-oriented environmental professions. The focus here was on the need for a multidisciplinary perspective that seeks to actively integrate the core methodological components of normative or practical reason into the education process. Beyond technical analysis, this perspective should be grounded in interpretive situational analysis, socio-political systems analysis, and environmental political philosophy. Inherent to this normative perspective would be an emphasis on bringing experts and citizens together in collaborative activities that could make good on the need for civic ecology, a missing component in the struggle for sustainability.

The discussion then suggested various strategies that could more practically link experts with the civic community, including public environmental education, environmental science shops, citizens' environmental juries, and collaborative inquiry. The goal is to bring together citizens and experts in ways that both promote civic ecology. At the same time, academic participants should be able to develop processes through which expert communities can facilitate citizen involvement to promote democratic decision making and more effective problem solving. Suggestions are offered both as a roadmap for curricular reforms and as a way for metropolitan universities to make good on the commitment to serve their surrounding communities.

References

Brundtland Commission. 1987. *Report of the Brundtland Commission: Our Common Future*. New York: Oxford University Press.

Bahro, R. 1987. *Avoiding Social and Ecological Disaster: The Politics of World Transformation* Nevada City, CA: Gateway Books.

Bast, Joseph l., Peter J. Hill, and Richard C. Rue. 1994. *Eco-Sanity: A common-Sense Guide to Environmentalism*. Silver Spring, MD: Madison Books.

Bowers, C. A. 1995. *Educating for an Ecologically Sustainable Culture*. Albany, NY: SUNY Press.

Brookfield, S. D. 1986. *Understanding and Facilitating Adult Learning*. San Francisco: Jossey-Bass.

Cordes, C. 1998. Community-Based Projects Help Scholars Build Public Support. *Chronicle of Higher Education,* April.

Dewey, J. 1927. *The Public and Its Problems.* New York: Swallow.

De Witt, J. 1994. Civic Environmentalism. Washington, DC: Congressional Quarterly Press.

Fischer, F. 1990. *Technocracy and the Politics of Expertise*. Thousand Oaks, CA: Sage.

Fischer, F. 1995. *Greening Environmental Policy: The Politics of a Sustainable Future*. New York: St. Martins Press.

Fischer, F. 2000. *Citizens, Experts, and the Environment: The Politics of Local Knowledge*. Durham, NC: Duke University.

Fischer, F. 2003. *Reaffirming Public Policy. New York City*. NY: Oxford University Press.

Freire, P. 1973. *Education for Critical Consciousness*. New York: Seabury Press.
Heron, J. 1996. *Co-operative Inquiry*. London: Sage.

Hills, M. and J. Mullett. 2000. *Community-Based Research. University Research:*

Collaborative Action for Health and Social Change. Victoria, BC: Community Health Promotion of Victoria Press.

Jorgensen, M. S., D. Hall, and I. Hall. 2004. How Can Science Schools Contribute to Governance. *Living Knowledge* No. 3, July: 7–10.

Joss, S., and J. Durant (eds.). 1995. *Public Participation in Science: The Role of Consensus Conferences in Europe*. London: Science Museum.

Kuhn, T.S. 1970. *The Structure of Scientific Revolutions*. Chicago: Chicago University Press

Lasswell, H. 1951. The Policy Orientation. In *The Policy Sciences*, H. Lasswell and D. Lerner (eds). Stanford: Stanford University Press.

Martell, L. 1994. *Ecology and Society*. Amherst: University of Massachusetts Press.

Morrision, R. 1995. *Ecological Democracy*. Boston: South End Press.

Ophuls, W. 1977. *Ecology and the Politics of Scarcity*. San Francisco: W.H. Freeman and Company.

Orr, D. 1992. *Ecological Literacy: Education and the Transition to a Postmodern World*. Albany: SUNY Press.

Rubin, C. T. 2002. Civic Environmentalism. In *Democracy and the Claims of Nature: Critical Perspectives for a New Century*, B. A. Minteer and B. P. Taylor (eds), 335 351. Lanham, Maryland: Rowman & Littlefield Publishers

Sclove, R. 1995. *Democracy and Technology*. New York: Guilford Press.

Shutkin, W. 2000. *The Land That Could Be: Environmentalism and Democracy in the 21st Century*. Cambridge, MA: MIT Press.

Sirianni, C. and L. Friedland. 2001. *Civic Innovation in American: Community Empowerment, Public Policy and the Movement for Civic Renewal*. Berkeley: University of California Press.

United Nations. 1992. *Rio Declaration on Environment and Development*. New York: United Nations.

Afterward
The Global State and Land Grant University of the 21st Century

The preceding chapters have shown clearly that our society is undergoing a profound transition. Having moved away from the agricultural age, it has shifted from an industrial to a knowledge-based society in an information age. Now may be time for state and land grant universities to craft a new social contract that provide the knowledge an educated metropolitan citizenry needs to achieve prosperity, security, and social well-being in the 21st century.

Perhaps it is constructive to revisit the land grant model in a way that may be embraced by all state and land grant universities if not all public institutions of higher education. The new state and land grant university moves us from the traditional notions of teaching, research, and service to language that encourages us to embrace learning, discovery, and engagement as the key components of a 21st century university. The new state and land grant university must provide access for the full diversity of America and lifelong learning for students. Discovery and engagement must be focused on the pressing educational, social, economic, scientific, and medical challenges of our time. Learning must be connected to engagement, and the research agenda must be broad and increasingly more interdisciplinary. The new state land grant university must also embrace a *global* perspective.

Change seems to be a constant in today's society and for tomorrow's future. Duderstadt (2000) observes: "Change will not only be the challenge to the American university, it will be the watchword for the years ahead. With change will come unprecedented opportunities for those universities with the vision, the wisdom, and the courage to lead in the century ahead." The Kellogg Commission (2000) admonishes that toward this end, the global state and land grant university of the 21st century must support:

o   Learning environments that meet the civic ends of public higher education by preparing students to lead and participate in a democratic society
o   Complex and broad-based agendas for discovery and graduate education that are informed by the latest scholarship and responsive to pressing public needs
o   Conscious efforts to bring the resources and expertise at our institutions to bear on community, state, national, and international problems in a coherent way

The global state and land grant university of the 21st century can provide the place and space for thinking about the future and fostering meaningful relationships between the university and American society. State and land grant universities are uniquely situated to accept this responsibility and exercise their *power to convene*. This power to convene is broad. It may convene scholars and students in traditional, professional, or executive education modes leading to degrees, certifications, or simply expanded awareness. It may convene researchers directly and through networks to address issues of concern by federal agencies and national research sponsors. It may convene scholars, professionals, public officials, and leaders in government, business, and interest groups as part of its outreach function.

Part of the challenge is assuring that convening is inclusive. Sustainability cuts across a variety of university programs. Being sure to include all units that may contribute to transformation is essential for long-term success. For instance, life-cycle cost accounting, eco-labeling, sustainable agriculture practices, ecological economics, industrial ecology, and others will play a critical role in the transformation that is needed and desired. The fields of civil, environmental, transportation, computer, electrical, mechanical, and electrical engineering; materials sciences; and biotechnology can generate the breakthroughs needed to achieve sustainability and resilience. Other critical players are the social science disciplines oriented toward behavioral change, systems analysis, institution building, and social and cultural understanding (i.e., communication, education, psychology, economics, sociology, science and technology studies, political science, history, cultural studies) as well as the arts and humanities that help us envision the quality of life we seek and wish to sustain for future generations (i.e., philosophy, language and literature, arts). Contributions and insights from these disciplines will not transform society unless the political, policy and planning practices are able to help build, sustain, and deploy institutions that advance civil society accordingly. Thus, new thinking about a sustainable metropolis must be interdisciplinary, informed by scholars from a broad range of academic disciplines and the planning and policy professions, and re-visioned as an emerging field moving beyond the past paradigms and the lens of single-discipline perspectives.

The appeal of "metropolitan sustainability" – or in the context of this book "metropolitan resilience" – is that it defines a very large heading under which many can gather, share ideas, and work together to shape significant contributions. The challenge is to ensure that the work that is done is meaningful and relevant both in today's society and for the future. The role of a global state and land grant university in convening and focusing energy on achieving a resilient metropolis has local, regional, and international significance. The challenge is to accept this responsibility and to act.

Karen P. DePauw
Mark McNamee
John Randolph

References

Duderstadt, James J. 2000. *A University for the 21st Century,* University of Michigan Press.

Kellogg Commission. 2000. *Renewing the Covenant: Learning, Discovery, and Engagement in a New Age and Different World.* Washington: National Association of State Universities and Land-Grant Colleges.